Body
of a
Dancer

Body
of a Dancer

Renée E. D'Aoust

etruscan press

For Enid ~ Love
who shares a
of movement and
of writing. May joy
always be present
in all your
creative pursuits!
with gratitude,
Renée

Rediscovered Books
Boise, Idaho
9 Feb. 2012

Etruscan Press
Wilkes University
84 West South Street
Wilkes-Barre, PA 18766
(570) 408-4546

www.etruscanpress.org

Published 2011 by Etruscan Press
Printed in the United States of America
Cover design by Starr Troup & Kanae Otsubo
Interior design and typesetting by Julianne Popovec
The text of this book is set in Minion Pro.

"Keeping Things Whole," from *Reasons for Moving; Darker; The Sargentville Notebook* by Mark Strand. Used by permission of Alfred A. Knopf, a division of Random House, Inc.

Cover photograph: Robert Schellhammer. Used by permission.

First Edition

11 12 13 14 15 5 4 3 2 1

Library of Congress Cataloging-in-Publication Data

D'Aoust, Renée E.
  Body of a dancer / Renée E. D'Aoust.
    p. cm.
  ISBN 978-0-9832944-1-2 (alk. paper)
  1. D'Aoust, Renée E. 2. Women dancers--United States--Biography. 3. Dance--Physiological aspects. 4. Martha Graham Dance Company. I. Title.
  GV1785.D266A3 2011
  792.802'8092--dc23
  [B]
                            2011034205

This book is printed on recycled, acid-free paper.

Body of a Dancer

Acknowledgments

Grateful acknowledgment is made to the editors of the following books, contests, and journals in which some of these essays first appeared: *Apollo's Lyre*, "Island Rose"; *The Bend*, "Body of a Dancer"; *Black Canyon Quarterly*, "Attending a Wedding: NYC"; *Cadillac Cicatrix*, "Theatrical Release"; *Keyhole*, "Audition # 99" and "Dancing in the Park"; *Mid-American Review*, "Graham Crackers," which was named a "Notable Essay" by *Best American Essays 2006* and won the Associated Writers Programs "Intro to Journals Project," Nonfiction Category; *Notre Dame Review*, "Holy Feet," which was named a "Notable Essay" by *Best American Essays 2010*; *Open Face Sandwich*, "Ballerina Blunders & a Few Male Danseurs," which was named a "Notable Essay" by *Best American Essays 2009*; *Redwood Coast Review*, "Daniela Can Fly"; and *Under the Sun*, "Attending a Wedding: Paris." I am grateful to Robert Gottlieb for including "Graham Crackers" in the anthology *Reading Dance*, which he edited (Pantheon Books, 2008).

Several authors and publishers granted fair use permission for quotations used within this text, and I would particularly like to thank and acknowledge the following: Joan Brady and her memoir *The Unmaking of a Dancer: An Unconventional Life*; Peter Kurth and his book *Isadora: A Sensational Life* (Little, Brown & Company); and Robert Greskovic for his marvelous resource *Ballet 101: A Complete Guide to Learning & Loving the Ballet*. Thank you to Frederick T. Courtright, President of The Permissions Company, Inc., who generously provided needed advice.

Numerous colleagues, editors, and friends provided support and suggestions during all stages of writing this book—thank you, all, including: Lois Adams, Mindy Aloff, Lisa Anderson, Leilani Arthurs, Alexandra Asbury, Janet Asbury, Peter Awn and Columbia University School of General Studies, Michael Bassett and Sandra Kaufmann, Mary Batten, Kate Baxter, Stefanie Batten Bland, Robert Bland, Carolyn Boschi, Beth Caldwell, Kathleen Canavan, Diana Capriotti, Sandy Compton, Uttara Asha Coorlawala,

Great Aunt Mary Cope, Debra Gail Courtney, Jo Dearsley, Tony D'Souza, Lloyd Duman and Loralee Haarr and the North Idaho College English Department, Judy Ellis, Stacey Engels, Pat Engstrom, Paul Engstrom, Danna Ephland, Julie Evans, Lynn Garafola, Katie Glasner, Anna Hardwick, Andrea Harris, Maggie Herold, Coleen Hoover, Stephen Kessler, Michael Kimball, Robert Kiwala, Claudia La Rocco, Maria Mercurio, Karen Michel, Carol Moldaw, Georges Montillet, Dinty W. Moore, Peter Mugavero, Patricia N. Nanon, Andi and Lance Olsen, Kunle Owolabi, Barbara Palfy, Abigail Palko's brother, Wendy Perron, Gloria Ray and Suzanne Sawyer and the East Bonner County Library District, David Reuther, Rhonda Rubinson, Rhoda Sanford, Dr. Dorothy E. Saxton, J.D. Schraffenberger, Marian Sherrett, the Sisters of the Holy Cross, John Sitter and Kate Raven, Janet Mansfield Soares and the Barnard College Department of Dance, Michael Steinberg, Truffle, the University of Notre Dame and the Notre Dame Creative Writing Program including MFA workshop members 2004-2006, the United States Postal Service including Cindy in Clark Fork and Junie in Hope, Rose and Bryan Wade, William Walsh, Thomas Warfield, Heidemarie Z. Weidner, Josh Weiss, Lili Yearsley Williams, Christopher Everett Wolf, Myra Woodruff, and Nancy Wozny. And to my teachers, with gratitude and affection, including: Mary Anthony, Wendy Arons, Dan Balaguy, Robert Battistini, W. Martin Bloomer, Susan Charlotte, Cornelius Eady, Austin Flint, Sonia Gernes, Sandra M. Gustafson, Flemming Halby, Alexis Hoff, Colette Inez, Ted McNeilsmith, Noël Mason, Marjorie Mussman, Nancy Rekow, Francia Russell, Valerie Sayers, Mark Slouka, J.T. Stewart, Steve Tomasula, Dale Worsley, and Kevin Wynn. Robert A. Ferguson read an early draft of the manuscript and continues to provide valuable direction and support; I extend my heartfelt gratitude for his friendship and love of all things lovely, including trees.

I am indebted to Nicholas Sparks for providing the Nicholas Sparks Fellowship to complete my MFA at the University of Notre Dame under the tutelage of my advisor William O'Rourke, who brought me to Notre Dame and lent a gentle eye to my work. While I was at Columbia University, the School of General Studies, Charles Bernstein, and the Helena Rubinstein Foundation provided needed scholarship support (thank you Skip Bailey!). Thank you to the Montana Dance Arts Association for providing a scholarship to attend the Graham Center for Contemporary Dance and the Graham Center for subsequent scholarship support. In addition, I wish to thank the Idaho Commission on the Arts and the Puffin Foundation for grants that supported writing projects, which invariably led to this book. I extend my thanks to Suzanne Carbonneau and the National Endowment of the Arts for a 2008 fellowship at the NEA Journalism Institute for Dance Criticism at the American Dance Festival.

I am particularly grateful to everyone at Etruscan Press for their joy in writing and publishing and everything in between, including Phil Brady, for reading this book so generously, Jim Cihlar, Robert Lunday, Erin Miele, Marissa Phillips, Julianne Popovec, and, for her luminescent guidance, Starr Troup.

All parents of dancers deserve special praise—no other art is as ephemeral and needs witnesses and, as Mark Morris says, "fabulous parents," as much as dance. Susan Saxton D'Aoust and Brian G. D'Aoust, my mother and father, drove me to daily ballet classes as a kid, bore witness to my New York modern dance life, and then watched me switch careers only to find themselves busy reading countless manuscript pages. You are loving and true. And every dancer should be so lucky to have big brothers: Anthony Frederick D'Aoust and Ian Lawrence D'Aoust have always applauded and continue to reflect my moral compass; thank you. Through walking, Daniele Puccinelli, my husband, taught me to waltz again. Truly, we are blessed.

Author's Note

With these recollections, I have taken some license with sequential time of dance events relating to my own personal history. In addition, I have changed a few names, identifying characteristics, and activities of some of the people to protect their privacy. The dance history of major figures and works contained herein should be considered factual. Any mistakes in that regard are my own.

Dedicated to Susan Saxton D'Aoust, my mother,
& Daniele Puccinelli, my husband,
with Gratitude & Love

Overture

"Practice means to perform, in the face of all obstacles, some act of vision, of faith, of desire. Practice is a means of inviting the perfection desired."

—Martha Graham

Body of a Dancer

Two years after Martha Graham died I stepped through the doors of Martha's House of Pelvic Truth in New York City. I didn't know it was called that then. All I knew was that I had to dance; training in the Graham technique—not to mention receiving a scholarship—seemed like the most direct route. My intuition was correct, but I neglected to realize that the route I chose may also have been the most damaging. As my spine straightened, my heart became buried deeper inside my body and desire began to reverse, curling in and around, twisting a love of movement into dedicated self-loathing. Martha Graham was still very much alive inside those walls; her ghost took hold of my senses, making me contract and move my body in ways I had previously thought impossible.

Grant, the grandson of our family friend Julie, said to me, "Remember why you came to the city—to dance—and do it. Then when you are done, remember to leave." He was an apparition who appeared at the beginning of my New York City dance career. Although Martha Graham entered my mind, I remembered Grant's advice. His voice stayed with me all the way, trying to drown out desperate desire with good common sense.

During the summer of 1993 in New York City, there was lamentation in the air. Martha Graham may have died of old age and a ruined liver, but now young people were dying. Lamentation was not for acts of terrorism, although the first World Trade Center bombing had just happened. Lamentation was everywhere for HIV and the plague of AIDS.

That fall after moving into a studio apartment on West 51st Street, I went to a performance by Elisa King's modern dance pick-up group, and the singer/piano player sang a threnody for his friend who had died of AIDS. These elegies were a common feature of city life—performances that wove cultural loss into artistic expression. That same singer would later play for classes at the Martha Graham Center for Contemporary Dance and be fired because of his voice. Too much sadness, perhaps. The director simply told him that he made too much noise.

In the fall of 1993 I attended a performance at a small church in the theatre district. I went alone, as I often did. My Montana dance teacher had recommended that I take Graham classes with Elisa King, but at this point Elisa wasn't available to the public because she was only teaching at the La-Guardia High School for the Performing Arts. Elisa had a beautiful breathy Graham movement so uncommon at the Graham Center itself. She wasn't rigid, and her body sang the joys of contraction without constipation.

When I first came to the city, my body was recovering from a serious back injury. I'd strained the lower back muscles of the erector spinae group doing the choreography of one of the teachers at the University of Montana while performing in a showcase at the American College Dance Festival. Gus Solomons jr. (he likes that lower-case "j") was judging, and the piece made it into the final performances. I spent most of the college festival on my back in a motel room in Ogden, Utah, thinking about taxes and spines. I literally could not move.

The teacher had been very nice—she'd given me flowers—but secretly I blamed her movement—*I blamed her*—for injuring my back. She incorporated spirals into and out of the floor in her choreography but gave no instruction on how to use the abdominal muscles to protect against over-twisting the back.

It's a common mistake of an amateur choreographer to expect a dancer to recreate movement by imitation rather than by technique. A choreographer doesn't have time to teach technique in rehearsal, but since dancers work for next to nothing, the least a beginning choreographer can do is not ruin a dancer's body.

After two months of inactivity, I auditioned for a summer scholarship to the Martha Graham Center of Contemporary Dance sponsored by the Montana Dance Arts Association. They'd brought in Myra Woodruff to adjudicate. Myra was currently in the Graham Company and later I heard she became Maurice Béjart's muse.

I won the scholarship everyone wanted: Graham. By then I wanted out of Montana. I'd moved there from Puget Sound in Washington State, which is where I was raised. In Montana I expected to marry a cowboy and live on a ranch. Lots of cowboys know how to dance, even if it is just line dancing. But, instead, in Big Sky country I found dance studios for the second time in my life and started moving my body. I also learned that quite often cowboys smell like manure and don't bathe as often as a girl would like. No cowboy. No ranch. All my time spent inside. I wanted to dance. My body had to move. My body could barely move.

The body of a dancer . . .

The body of a dancer is tired before it is worn out. The back fails. The adductors fail. The neck muscles are too loose. The neck muscles are too tight. The extension is too low. The extension is never high enough. The body of a dancer has an ache in the right ankle. Or the right big toe. Or maybe the dancer fell and hurt the coccyx and bruised the tail.

"Remember the tail," says the first dance teacher, trying to get her students to lengthen their backs, to stand up straight. "You still have a tail," she'll say to her class of eight-year-olds, "so use it!"

The body of a dancer . . .

The body of a dancer has an ache in her abdomen. The doctor has never seen such abdominal muscles. He's never seen such a loosey-goosey, leggy person before. He's never seen someone so thin. The dancer doesn't have anorexia. Not most anyway. Most have control. That's different. If they eat a bagel, never with butter or cream cheese, they toast it because they believe toasting gets rid of the starch.

The body of a dancer . . .

The body of a dancer has shin splints up the front of the leg. She has a bunion from her years as a ballet dancer before she became a modern dancer. She has no toenails. Now as a modern dancer, she has floor burns up and down her spine. She has skin splits on the bottoms of her feet, and she wraps the splits with Elastacon, an expensive medical tape sometimes used on horses. The pharmacy on Eighth Avenue and 53rd carries Elastacon for modern dancers and for all the Broadway gypsy dancers.

To this day, I can tell you the injuries of all my friends. I can tell you their physical problems more than I can tell you their family history. I can tell you that my friend Stef has trouble with her neck and sometimes with a knee. I can tell you that my friend Heather injured her calf muscle and that she was terrified because she'd never had an injury before. She didn't know what the rest of us were talking about when we said a strained muscle hurt so badly. I can tell you my friend Mara had trouble with her lower back. I can tell you about another friend who had a herniated disk and spent six immovable months on her back. The doctors told her she would never dance again, and she told me she couldn't imagine her life without dance. I can tell you almost everyone at Graham had trouble with their lower backs. I can tell you my friend Sandra occasionally has a glitch in her hip. I can tell you about a young woman named Kathleen who was slated for the New York City Ballet Company whose teacher ripped out the muscles in her right hip area because he forced the leg to her ear to show her she wasn't working hard enough. That teacher was Perry Brunson. He was an amazing teacher. Placement, alignment, discipline. We lost him all those years ago. That was at the beginning of AIDS. We didn't say AIDS back then.

Pain . . .

Don't tell anyone about the aches and pains. The body of a dancer is a perfect instrument. It is honed. Even when it shows the effort with modern dance, done barefoot, as opposed to defying gravity in ballet, done in pointe shoes, the body is still a tool, an instrument, an expression of the soul. And if the soul isn't interesting. . . forget it.

The body, Martha Graham says, *never lies.*

My body lied all the time. The tiny spot on the front right of my hip, on the top of my iliac crest, was on fire by the end of my dancing life. I couldn't let anyone touch it; the pain sent my face grimacing, involuntarily. I didn't tell anyone I used to spend days in bed or on the floor, trying to get my lower back to release various spasms. In rehearsal, I often wore a flexible neoprene back brace. There was Velcro on one side, and I wrapped it tightly around my lower back. The neoprene held my sacrum together. I covered it with a floppy sweatshirt.

Drugs . . .

My boyfriend Chris followed me from Montana to New York City, and he would bring me aspirin while I lay in bed or on the floor. Then we tried ibuprofen. We settled on naproxen, using the product Aleve.

I remember Chris begging me to lift weights, to try some toning exercises for my muscles, to rethink the way I was training my body. He also told me to lose weight—I was 5'5" and 112 pounds—and he pissed me off so much, I didn't do anything else he suggested. I should have. Maybe I would still be dancing.

Maybe not.

They say there are three kinds of dancers: 1. Those who dance when young and never dance again; 2. Those who dance professionally and move on; and 3. Those who dance professionally and then move on into careers in dance, teaching, and/or choreography.

My own personal opinion is that there is a fourth kind of dancer: for her, dance never leaves the heart; dance is the purest expression of life; it is movement without voice, movement that is a gift of the body.

Renée E. D'Aoust

The mind . . .

The modern dancer's mind is just as twisted as the ballet dancer's mind. She thinks she is too tall, too short, too fat, too thin (oops, never too thin), too blonde, too brunette, too pale, too dark, too, too, too something to be a dancer. She is wrong for the part. She is not wrong for the part. Her body is wrong for the part. But her body is *her.* There is absolutely no difference. Her body is the instrument, and she is the instrument.

When I moved to New York City in the summer of 1993, I wanted to get trained. Then, I thought, I'll see what I want to do with a trained body. I was twenty-five-years old. Old for a dancer. Even a modern dancer. After eight years training in ballet as a kid, I'd left ballet at the age of sixteen. I declared I wanted a broader focus to my life, but it was also true that I had started to realize I would not become a principal or even a soloist, and I didn't want to be part of the corps. Maybe in a different era, Margot Fonteyn's era, I could have made principal. Danced *Swan Lake.* Maybe not. For a while after ballet, a broader focus took over. I finished high school, then traveled, held different jobs, and briefly went to university without completing a degree. I had the opportunity to come back and dance again. Myra Woodruff gave me the chance.

New York City. I was willing to bleed for my art. But I wasn't willing to die for it. I made a distinction in my mind because I'd seen death at the Pacific Northwest Ballet School. I'd seen a woman who was skin and bones, a woman who was a warning to my dancing life. I'd seen her, and I remembered her. I never knew her name, but I saw each rib. I saw her collar bones. I saw the protrusion of each vertebra. She had no pubic hair.

I'd seen the hollows of her eyes. She had looked me directly in the eye in the dressing room. I was ten years old. She must have been sixteen or eighteen or maybe even twenty. She'd looked at me, and I had stared back, and I had heard her words in my head, "I am dying." I remembered.

My mother had seen this girl, too, and delayed my enrollment at the Pacific Northwest Ballet School for an entire year because of it. My mother figured that if there was a skeleton walking around Pacific Northwest Ballet, it was not the sort of dance school she wanted her daughter to attend. Instead, I enrolled at the Cornish School of the Arts and trained with Noël Mason, who had danced with the Joffrey Ballet. When Ms. Mason moved from Cornish to Pacific Northwest Ballet School a year later, I followed. For the next three years after that, I was "Clara" in *The Nutcracker*—Michael Smuin's version, not the Kent Stowell and Maurice Sendak version.

Francia Russell, the director of the school, said to me, "You're perfect for 'Clara,' because you are much more of an actress than a dancer."

It was a condescending compliment. I couldn't handle her honesty, but I did appreciate it. That's why, at sixteen, when Francia Russell told me the most I could hope for as a ballet dancer was as a corps member in some Midwestern third-tier company, I decided to quit. My excuse was that I would act. But really, something inside died. An ex-dancer knows what I mean. When I left ballet, I left my identity. None of my dance classmates phoned. I had succumbed to failure. I did not have the biology. My extension was not high enough. I had breasts. I would never be a ballet dancer. I was nothing.

At the age of twenty-five, I had a lot to prove as a modern dancer. But I had placement and turn-out and good arches and musicality and presence. Ballet had given me all that. I was ready—in modern—to learn. I worked harder than all my classmates. I had lost years. I couldn't waste a second.

In the summer of 1993, I felt I'd been given a second chance. I was home. In my body. In the body of a dancer. Or what would soon be the body of a dancer. There was much to do: shape the thighs; get the turn-out working again; get the extension going; develop strength; balance. And jump. And land without hopping. God, I loved to jump. To leap. To fly to the sky and never ever land. To take to the heavens. The blue expanse holds me there.

The spirit . . .

The spirit can be broken, but not from an aching body. The spirit is broken because often the dancer's dream is unattainable. The dancer dreams of being a star. There are very few stars in the dance world. Very few. This realization dawns slowly.

And then the pain sets in. And the pain sets in deeper. And you keep dancing because you must, because you realize you are a gambler, and you realize if you cannot get that split fall just right you will never succeed at life. If your *plié* does not improve, and quick, you will fail in the world. Your center is working overtime, and you do not hear reason. There is no reason. Only movement. A certain psychosis takes over. You are willing to move and to move and to move.

So I moved in the dance studios of Martha Graham. I began contracting. The Graham contraction hollows out the abdomen so that it looks like a sail filled with air. The spine is the webbing of the sail and the legs are the ropes. I contracted.

I didn't listen to reason. I ingested four Aleve tablets a day. I took Tums. I placed Chinese plasters over my lower back, rubbed Tiger Balm Extra Strength on my hips, took an Epsom salt bath every night, massaged my feet without oil—you want tough, hard skin—and wore sweatpants to bed even in summer.

I felt that my heart could encompass the sky because I was home in a dancer's body. There was no place else I wanted to be.

Act One

"One began a spiral fall by pivoting on both feet while leaning back and contracting on bent knees, descending and turning simultaneously until the shoulders grazed the floor and one came to rest on one's back. The element of excitement was supplied by the fraction of a second during which the body was totally off balance and falling. One recovered by reversing the process, jackknifing, circling forward, and rising to stand erect."

—Agnes de Mille,
Martha: The Life and Work of Martha Graham

Graham Crackers

The first day of the Martha Graham Center for Contemporary Dance Summer Intensive, there is a large spot of dried and crusted blood in the center of the main studio floor. Advanced dancers doing sparkles on the diagonal across the floor jump before the blood and land afterward.

"Take to the air," yells Pearl Lang. She is petite, elderly, full of spine. Her gray-black hair is pulled with a small pink bow into a small chignon at the base of her neck.

One barefoot young woman lands smack on the crusted blood. Claire is usually a very careful, very precise dancer. The entire line of dancers, each waiting a turn, cringes.

Although the floor and center exercises took up an hour and a half of the two-hour class, no one cleaned up the blood. Kristi is absent. Kristi doesn't mind cleaning up blood and sometimes checks the studio floor before class. Spilled blood is a regular occurrence in a Graham class. Since modern dancers dance barefoot, often the skin tears or burns from the pressure of contact with the floor. If there's blood, Kristi gets the rubbing alcohol and paper towel and wipes the floor. She never uses gloves. Kristi also goes barefoot at Grateful Dead concerts.

It is a bold move to be absent for the first day of Summer Intensive, especially when company auditions will take place at the end of the six-week session. Absence means weakness. Survival of the fittest is taken to new heights in the Graham School. You must not simply survive. You must thrive or perish. If you perish, it's your own fault. The lipid content of your cellular structure is your fault, too.

Art won't come to the weak. And art isn't authentic if it doesn't bleed. In other fields—take the visual arts, for example—young people haphazardly and loosely refer to themselves as artists before they even know what it means to be touched by fire—as if without practice and guts and pain, they are already exalted simply because they label themselves artists. But at Graham, no pain means no gain. I dare you to toss around the word *artiste* lest you rot in hell for your audacity.

It takes ten years to make a dancer, says Martha.

Martha has been dead for two years, but Summer Intensive is still sacred: Pearl Lang teaches the composition class. It happens right after technique class. The dancers make up stupid twisty movements and call the amalgamation of their favorite moves choreography. Always one idiot dancer puts in a *grand jeté*—legs split, leaping high across the floor—and always Pearl takes it out.

"Yes dear," Pearl says, "I know you love to leap, but show me something you don't love to do, and make it original."

Pearl speaks kindly because, usually, the girl has no talent. Pearl does not speak kindly to those with talent. It's a given. If you can't take it, get out. This girl, Fran, will become an arts administrator, and then she'll marry a wealthy banker named Ted who works on Wall Street for Merrill Lynch. Pearl knows not to alienate money and the financial support of the arts. Fran might even think she could have made it. Usually the untalented in any field are unrealistic that way.

Pearl calls the short pieces "compositions," but the dancers call their pieces "choreography." They pronounce the "ch" as in "chore," so the word "choreography" sounds as odd as the little squirmy dance pieces look. No matter. The dancers know the pieces look odd, and they know they look like fools flailing about center floor, but they also know the little pieces of "choreography" are just a practice exercise, like copying a famous painting into a sketch book. But there's no framed picture hanging on the wall of Martha's studio; instead, there's just sweat in the air and blood on the floor. Lots of dancers have bodies that resemble gorgeous frames hanging in the Metropolitan Museum of Art—but not the Met where Leo will end up as a has-been dancing in the Metropolitan Opera Ballet. There are plenty of dancers with beautiful bodies but no passion within. Some have ugly bodies, too. That's why they study Graham.

In Martha's studio, there is the scarred and ancient grand piano in the corner, the double doors that open to Martha's courtyard and her tree, the high narrow windows, fluorescent lights and fan overhead, and the old barre with braces that are pulling off the wall.

The braces on the barre really need to be fixed. The barre cannot withstand the pull of weight for much longer. One brace has a screw loose, so part of it hangs limply off the wall. Ostensibly dancers don't pull on the barre, but that is ballet. This is Graham. In Graham, dancers use the barres to pull away, to find the arch in the side of the body where one side swoops in and the other side swoops out, or to find the contraction. For that ever-present search, you face the barre, both hands on it, and pull back away from it, pretending someone punched you right in the gut—hard—whoosh, all the breath comes out of you, and you double over in pain and agony and glory and beauty. Back in Martha's day, teachers would punch you in the gut to be sure you knew the real feeling. Real feeling. Real sensation. Art is no substitute for the real.

"You're a bird, an eagle," the teacher, Jacqulyn Buglisi, screams, "let go of the barre. Fly!"

Several dancers actually let go of the barre and fall on their butts. They are the ones who always follow directions, especially when screamed in high pitch. If you hadn't been so terrified of Ms. Buglisi, you might have laughed: The ceiling is too low for flying anywhere, soon the barre will pull completely off the wall, and the humidity is so great that by the middle of class you want to plop down to the floor like the idiot dancers who actually let themselves fall on their tailbones when they didn't have to do it. Ms. Buglisi had, of course, been speaking metaphorically.

When she describes a ceremony of Native Americans who hung by their pectoral muscles in the sun, she does not specify the tribe. They wove rawhide on either side of the muscle, so the body of the muscle took the weight of the body, and then they hung from poles. "Praise the sky!" whispers Buglisi, her face ecstatic at the thought of suffering. By the end of her class, you don't care if you sink into a little puddle of sweat: Your suffering is that great.

Again and again, you dutifully turn and face the barre the way you face a partner. The heterosexual male dancers in Graham have to be tough—if they're not, they'll be used up. Though, of course, a male partner isn't necessarily heterosexual, the role of the male in Graham is understood to be heterosexual or animal—Jason in *Cave of the Heart*, the Minotaur in *Errand into the Maze*—even if performed by a homosexual. Primarily the men function as hunks of flesh, the catalyst for the leading lady's freedom—she works against him, she hits him, she loves him; always, in the end, she spits him out. She is warrior. He is dirt. The barre has to be as solid as a man, as sturdy as a partner should be, but the studio is old, the plaster peeling, and the barre is pulling away from the wall from years of stress and abuse.

You grab the barre and pull away, the way Martha herself might have grabbed Erick Hawkins if she wasn't slapping him, your butt tight and head bowed, your back curving and your abdomen hollowed out. Please let this class be over soon, you think. In Graham, you hardly ever get to use the barre so hanging on for dear life should be a treat.

The class where you hang on the barre is an anomaly. Graham class starts off with excruciating floor work, and the spine is supposed to be unnaturally straight, straighter than a heterosexual, so straight it looks like a Giacometti rendition of a woman in shock. All those little bronze bits are the sweat balls rolling off the body. What you don't know is that the emphasis on the straight spine in the Graham technique means that over time the natural curves of the cervical, thoracic, and lumbar regions flatten out so the spine eventually looks like a board. It means that the center of the body falls lower than in ballet technique, and it means that many Graham dancers in training flail about because the spine is rigid. That rigidity makes the arms stick out like scarecrows. No wonder everyone in Graham is looking for a center. How can you find a center if you have such distorted placement?

"We're living a long way from Bumfuck, Kansas, now, girls," Amanda announces in her British accent to the dressing room after class. She is taking off her sweat-soaked leotard and tights, exchanging them for a Lycra unitard hand sewn by Arturo. The dressing room is a long, thin room on the second floor of the Graham Center. "Where the hell is Kristi to wipe up that blood?" Amanda is black and has no boobs, and she is very thin and tall. She has attitude. But she also has passion. She'll get into the Graham Company. The Company needs a black girl this year.

Kristi went to visit her sister in Hawaii and phoned to say her plane had been delayed, but nobody believed her. Everyone suspects she stayed in Hawaii with her sister to smoke some more pot on the beach and soak up the sun. Deadheads are potheads. Everyone knows she isn't coming back. They are glad. One down.

But Amanda says, "There's always another to take her place." Except there isn't. If you consider it, life doesn't refill people who go missing. Kristi couldn't stick it out, and now the question is who will willingly take on the role of wiping up spilled blood in the center of the room before Pearl Lang's composition class. The dancers, like monks, are in charge of cleaning their own space, their own temple, but no one wants to do it. No one wants to touch HIV-positive blood. You know all dancers are promiscuous; it's a given.

This Summer Intensive there are dancers from Croatia and Brazil, Germany and Texas. There are a few from Oklahoma because a former Graham Company member works at the University of Oklahoma School of Dance. Other states are represented, too. There are no dancers from the

African continent. Amanda is from Great Britain. There are three from Taiwan. Kun-Yang is one of them, but he won't make the Company because of his height. He's too short. There are four from Brazil. Six from Italy. Italians really love Graham. The American dancers say the Italians love Graham's pathos: her abdominal contraction. The Italian dancers say the Americans love Graham's control: her stately walk. The Italian men love sleeping with the American men, and the American women want to sleep with the Italian men.

Briget pulls on a new leotard. She wears a fresh one for each class. She always smells like Downy or Bounce. Briget has been at the school for ten years. She is a legend: "That girl who auditions for the Company every year." Someday she'll get in, even though she is too stiff and too tall, because persistence pays off. When Briget dances she looks like a sunflower that never should have tried to sway in the wind in the first place—as if a sunflower has any control over weather. No dancer has control over management, especially if half of management thinks Graham wanted all her dances to die with her and half thinks the reverse. But management in a dance company just means those who yell the loudest and are the most intimidating and have been around the longest. All the dancers are waiting for Briget's right knee to bust out. Briget's right leg wobbles on every landing. But she'll get in her beloved company first, and then her knee will bust out. Another one down.

Persistence really does pay off. If Carol Fried knows she can't break you, then she'll take you. The trouble is, most people go crazy along the way and stop dancing entirely. Daniela became the Firebird and tried flying out her fifth-story studio apartment window. Shelley understudied the role of Jason's princess, murdered by Medea in *Cave of the Heart*, and then actualized the role with a twist by murdering herself with poison. Shelley didn't even need Medea to do the dirty work. Through death, Jason's princess loses her ability to speak—though probably she never had that ability in the first place—and Shelley lost her ability to speak, too. Sometimes a dancer just plain old loses it.

The other dancers call it going crackers, and if you stay around the

Graham School it will happen to you, too. So get your training and get out before you become stiff and rigid and unmusical and forget your reasons for moving in the first place. When a dancer becomes a bird or something bad happens, the dancers say, "Ah, nuts." It means, "Good, another dancer out of the way"; or, "She went nuts"; or even, "Ah nuts, it could have been me." Male dancers don't go crazy. Their penises are too needed. Often the males are homosexuals and too sweet to go crazy. It isn't in them.

In the dressing room, Amanda says it the most plainly: "Kristi couldn't take it." The dancers all nod. They can take it.

Dancers are not known for speech, which is nonetheless interesting because speech and text are very important attributes in the postmodern world of dance. David Dorfman thinks he's a choreographer and a writer, but really he simply used to be a baseball player, so he knows how to squat real well. Most dancers in the downtown scene don't have any technique, and they don't have any speech, either. The text they say is "I saw my mother" or something deep like that, and the audience is supposed to say, "Oh, wow, intense," or something deep like that. Text scrolls across a screen in something Stephen Petronio dreamed up, which looks like a scrolling message in Times Square, except it is so small and so weird and so out of place, hanging there above the stage like the Stonehenge replica in the movie *This is Spinal Tap,* that the text means nothing at all. Neither does the dance. And the real Stonehenge is all surrounded by cement, for that matter. Who wants to dance on cement?

Dance critics think text means something and give it credence as such, but like all critics they think that everything means something even if it doesn't. Sometimes a dancer doing stupid twisty movements and speaking nonsensical text is just a dancer speaking bad text. It isn't to say that Martha wouldn't have tried techno-gadgets had she still been alive, but techno-gadgets only go so far if the dancers have nothing else to do—or, worse, if they look as if they have nothing else to do. Techno-gadgets can't help a sloppy dancer or a fat one or one without any technique. Techno-realism can't make stupid twisty movements anything other than what they are. Go ahead and yell: RELEASE TECHNIQUE IS TECHNIQUE. You know it isn't. That's why Pina Bausch uses amazing dancers, trained dancers with technique, even if they only stand still or walk around in a Bausch ballet or open their legs wide and close them. Hieronymus Bosch would have adored Pina. For sure.

The spine is your body's tree of life, says Martha.

One! You're down. Two! Scoot your feet around and under and wrench yourself up to standing, don't feel the tear across your knee, ignore it, it isn't happening. Three! You're up.

"And again!" Pearl yells.

Don't think because you haven't been taught to think. Do it. Whatever they want. Again and again. All art is the act of showing up. You've been taught that a dancer lives to dance: Movement to a dancer is like breathing to mortal souls. You must bleed. Bleed now!

You've heard it so many times it doesn't matter if you believe it yourself. The body is aching, but you don't feel it now. You'll feel it later when you can barely lift a hand to turn the faucet on to fill the bathtub with water, and you can barely lift the box of Epsom salts and pour it into the tub. Whatever gender you are sleeping with at the time brought home the Epsom salts. Special treat. You dump the whole box into the bath and the carton falls in, too, because you're so tired you didn't hold it tightly enough. There is only tomorrow in the world of dance because goals are too far out of reach, so use up everything now.

Somehow you lift your leg over the rim of the tub, and though earlier in the day you could fall to the floor in one count, now it takes you eight counts to get your body lowered into the water. You sit holding your knees crunched up to your chest in a little huddle. It hurts too much to lean back, so you just sit there in a little ball in the water. If you are lucky, your sexual partner comes into the bathroom and clucks a little and picks up a washcloth and washes your back. Gently. Ever so gently.

After the bath, you don't have sex; you never have sex. You are too tired to have sex, and too sore to have sex and who the hell wants to explore the body at night when you've been exploring the body all day and you know where every little muscle is that isn't doing what it should? Those piriformis muscles would be great for sex because they are so strong, but you can feel your sciatic nerve ever so slightly. The last thing you want is for someone to touch you and make the nerve go on fire.

The words of the raunchier Graham teachers yelling at you reverberate in your brain all night as you lie there and stare at the ceiling: "Have an orgasm! Then you'll know life. None of you know life! Where is your contraction? Where is your orgasm? You're all frigid!"

Only the lucky ones have sex, the chosen ones, as Martha would say, "the athletes of the gods." These are the true purveyors of Martha's House—the House of Pelvic Truth. It isn't called that for nothing. Somehow the athletes of the gods are able to make all the little muscles work in their body and fall to the floor and breathe while they contract and then run and leap and look as if they do nothing but live life fully and completely in their bodies and in the dance. They have orgasms at night with a lover from a country foreign to their own. The rest just open the legs. That isn't even sex.

There is no question the will is always there—even in your bed at night, even if you just open your legs—the will to move with power and force and beauty. Martha says she never sought beauty, even though the grotesque is beautiful. When the teacher walks into Martha's studio all the students stand, quickly, and pull the feet together and squeeze the buttocks together and keep the arms long, palms in against the thighs, hopefully the thighs are not feeling or looking too big this morning, the hair should already be pulled tightly back and away from the face—it is okay if it's in a ponytail, no bun-heads here, though you might act like one.

One! You're up, standing, for the teacher. "Please sit," Pearl says, sometimes offering a little bow. Two! You sit. "And," she says. The pianist begins banging out whatever he's banging out this morning, and you are bouncing up and down, pushing your head to your feet: bounce, bounce, bounce. "Breathings!" yells Pearl. You breathe. Then stop breathing. This is how you start every day. For blood. For art. For Martha.

Act Two

"You put a man and woman on a stage together, and already it's a story."

—George Balanchine,
Quoted in Robert Greskovic's
Ballet 101: A Complete Guide to Learning & Loving the Ballet

Attending a Wedding: NYC

A t the start of the ceremony, when the music paused, I turned off the fluorescent lights in the bathroom and opened the door. Through the crack between the door and the wall, I had a full view of the main room. My scholarship at Graham only covered tuition. I had to work to cover living expenses.

The groom wore a tuxedo not unlike my own. Short, he had blonde hair and brown eyes. He looked similar to the men I saw standing on the subway platform at the Fulton Street stop when I came to work: He lacked natural color, his eyes had bags of blue underneath, and his complexion was well manicured with money. He looked harried, as if he were worried about getting a spot on the Number 6 Train uptown, and his hands looked as if they were better occupied holding the *Wall Street Journal* than waiting for the palm of his future wife.

The string quartet started playing "Here Comes the Bride." The groom adjusted his bow tie and turned to watch the bride. His best man, equally well manicured but taller, put his hand on the groom's shoulder.

The cummerbund felt loose around my waist. It did not fit properly, so I had tied the narrow ends of the cummerbund around a belt loop at the back of the black pants. The shirt, also too big, bagged around my waist. I let the bathroom door close slowly, softly, and reached around to tighten the cummerbund. The shirt came from the Velvet Underground, a second-hand store. The tuxedo itself came from Tuxedo and Sons Wholesale.

25

"I've been in the Tux industry a long time, and they don't come small enough for you," said the man who fit me. There were three men sitting in the back of the tux place when I walked in on a Saturday morning to buy the outfit. They looked like a retired group from the Mafia.

"Catering job?" asked the one with a bald head. He didn't ask it unkindly, but it was clear he'd seen a line of people coming through his store to buy tuxes for work—not marriage.

My whole tuxedo outfit was makeshift, making me feel disheveled, inefficient and small. Small and fat. Not small and perky. A self-loathing of my body ran through everything I did: dance, work, sex. No, sometimes I lost myself when I opened my legs. Rarely. But sometimes.

Before beginning work, the freelance staff of South Street Seaport Catering had gathered for the nightly meeting. Probably none of the two dozen or more people assembled for their paying jobs as food servers, bartenders, coat check attendants, or doormen had enough money to consider being married at the Seaport. The lights across the Brooklyn Bridge shone into the room, making the whole wedding setting magical.

Still, South Street Seaport definitely would not be my first choice for a wedding location even if marriage looked like a promising part of my future, which it didn't, and even if I could afford it, which I couldn't. I wanted to say I probably couldn't ever afford it, but that wasn't part of my current emphasis on positive thinking. I'd been reading *Creative Visualization* by Shakti Gawain and visualizing myself on the dance stage: perfect balance, no wobbles, perfect leg extension to my ear, perfect body, one-hundred pounds.

I found out about the catering company, which preferred employees who were actors, dancers, painters, or writers, through my friend Heather, who also studied at Graham. During my interview, as soon as I said I was a dancer, the manager Tom said, "You got the job. Get yourself a tux."

Tom placed me in the bathroom. *A bathroom attendant girl,* I thought. My positive future had not included such jobs.

ℰᴑ

On my way to the bathroom earlier in the evening, I had run directly into the bride. I had quickly inclined my head downward the way English maids do on Masterpiece Theatre. Pretending to relay a message to the very thin and very petite bride, I used the third-person: "The bride will find the bridal changing room down this hall and to the right."

A bridesmaid in a skin-tight peach-colored silk dress, showing bones, no curves, and no breasts waited as the bridal entourage, including four other flat-chested women wearing peach dresses, moved away down the hallway.

"Thank you," said the bride's friend. Her accent sounded Midwestern. Her voice was flat, but there was a slight twang that sounded out of place in an urban bridal party.

"You're welcome. My pleasure," I said, valiantly trying to maintain the veneer that I knew how to be a maidservant.

"Beth, hurry up," called one of the bridesmaids.

Beth clicked away in peach-colored stilettos.

When I first entered the bathroom, my thick-soled black leather shoes had squeaked on the white-tiled floor. The room had vertical pink and white striped wallpaper three quarters of the way up the wall. A thin strip of flowered wallpaper, in a lilac color, separated the stripes from pink paint on the rest of the wall.

Although it was already clean, I wiped the mirror with Windex. I looked in each of the four toilet bowls. Checked the toilet paper. Checked the Kleenex boxes on the counter. Straightened the silver tray on one side of the counter. On the tray were individually wrapped combs in plastic, a can of hair spray, a tube of styling mousse, a small jar of clear nail polish, packages of aspirin and antacid tablets, and a glass jar of mints.

Someone, probably Tom's efficient assistant Sheila, had shoved white lilies into a crystal vase and placed it between the two sinks. The petals were crushing each other.

Not a good way to begin a marriage, I thought. *Crushing prevents the sweet scent.*

The lilies had a faint smudge of pink through the center of the aromatic white petals. I pulled a few stalks higher than the others, filling the bathroom with a fresh, sticky smell, which reminded me of my friend Paula's old-fashioned garden back in Montana. I used one of the linen hand towels to collect the yellow pollen from the pistils of the flowers, which had fallen on the counter. The pollen left yellow blotchy stains on the towel.

My cummerbund adjusted, I re-opened the door a crack. There were about a hundred people in the main room. The bridesmaids in their peach outfits stood at the front of the room. The bride was walking down the aisle. She held her head still. Directly in front of her white satin gown she held, equally still, a bouquet of white roses. There was an intricate lace pattern that scrolled around her tiny waist. Trails of lace with pearls at each end rested on top of the full-length satin gown. A veil of the same lace covered the bride's face. There was no bridal train and no flower girl. The bride walked alone. Acting as stage floodlights, the lights of the Brooklyn Bridge lighted her way down the aisle. The whizzing headlights of the endless traffic racing through the early winter night were shooting stars.

I wish upon a star, I thought, but the thought trailed off. *Where is the bride's father?*

The string quartet had stopped playing. I watched the bride's back as she faced the altar. The groom did not touch his bride.

"We are gathered today," said the minister, "for the wedding of Jonathan Atkins, the Third, and Abigail Lili Shepherd."

I remembered my friend Paula's wedding down the Bitterroot Valley in Montana just before I received the Montana Dance Arts Association scholarship to the Graham Summer Intensive. I had no idea then that I would audition for the two-year program at Graham and receive a scholarship and move permanently to New York City.

At Paula's wedding, her father, proudly wearing his Stetson, had walked his daughter down the path by the Bitterroot River, past her old-fashioned garden of lilies, and up the meadow to an arbor covered in honeysuckle. The groom's best men all wore cowboy hats, and the bridesmaids all had honeysuckle, a tender, delicate flower, woven through their hair. When the husband and wife kissed under the arbor, we had all whistled and clapped and hollered.

I saw a glint of gold, or maybe platinum, as this bride and groom exchanged rings.

"I now pronounce you man and wife," said the minister. He didn't wear a collar and could just as likely have been a justice of the peace. He could have been a non-denominational something.

"You may kiss the bride," he said.

The crowd was still and silent. The kiss, short and soundless.

The string quartet started playing Bach's "Brandenburg Concerto," I wasn't sure which one, and the couple turned to face their audience. The groom still appeared more suited to a board meeting than to his own wedding. The bride squeezed her lips together as if she had just applied lipstick.

As they walked down the aisle, the new husband and wife kept their eyes fixated on the back of the room. The groomsmen started shaking hands with the guests while the bridesmaids kissed the guests' cheeks. I could smell the buffet in the adjacent dining room.

I moved away from the bathroom door and switched on the lights. I sat down on a wrought-iron vanity chair next to the counter and held ready a hand towel for someone to take from my hands.

"I'll just use the restroom," said one of the peach-colored bridesmaids as she entered the bathroom. She emptied the contents of her Chanel makeup bag on the counter. She retouched her blue eyes with a Clinique charcoal-colored liner pencil, then brushed a shimmering, silver eye shadow by MAC on her lids. Her makeup had not faded, and when she reapplied it, the colors didn't look any heavier.

Perhaps good makeup absorbs into the skin, I thought, *and bad makeup reapplied just looks embalmed.* Many years ago in high school my friend Erika had reapplied makeup at every break so that by the end of the day she looked ready for a chorus part in *Don Giovanni.* This woman looked ready for the runway. She nodded at me as she left the room.

Gradually, the bathroom became a gathering place. Women chatted to each other while in the stalls or at the counter. "Isn't Abi a beautiful bride?" asked one bridesmaid. "I'm glad she waited," answered her friend.

"It's so special," said another, directly to me as she picked the towel out of my hands.

"Yes, wonderful," I said.

"No tip jar?" the woman asked.

"Not necessary, but thank you," I answered.

"Well, here." The woman leaned over and tucked a bill right into my pocket. "I used to be an art student. I know."

For a moment the bathroom was empty. Through the closed door, I could hear that a swing band had replaced the string quartet. Dancing had started. I took the bill out of my pocket. A twenty. That would cover a week of subway rides.

A woman with bobbed hair, wearing a sequined, silver gown, came into the restroom. Even though every hair looked in place, she tore off the plastic around one of the combs and passed it through her hair. It made no difference. Every hair still looked in the same place. She had an enormous diamond ring on her finger. The bathroom lights sparkled off the diamond ring and the sequins on her gown.

"It's my engagement ring," she said, looking at me watching her in the mirror. I didn't realize I'd been staring—ogling her ring, her poise. "My fiancé couldn't come tonight. Used to date the bride."

"It's a beautiful ring," I said.

"Yes," said the woman. She threw the comb in the garbage can and walked out. She wasn't a good shot, though, and the comb missed the can. I got up and threw the comb away.

The manager's assistant Sheila, wearing a headset to coordinate the timing of the evening, entered the bathroom.

"Holding up?" she asked.

"Thanks. Fine." I was glad I'd been standing when Sheila walked in rather than sitting. I wanted to be moved out of the bathroom and up to serving hors d'oeuvres. I'd make $15 an hour instead of $10.

"You dancers are always good on your feet. Don't forget to get food later before you leave. *Gratis*." She spoke rapidly.

"Thanks."

"Perk of a corporate wedding. The raspberry chocolate truffle cake rocks."

Immediately after Sheila left, a middle-aged woman entered the bathroom. Beth, the friendly bridesmaid who had spoken to me earlier in the evening, followed. As soon as the door shut, the older woman put both arms up on the wall as if to steady herself. She wore a cream-colored linen suit with a peach silk shirt that matched the bridesmaids' dresses. The suit fit her well, but the linen had wrinkled.

"He doesn't love her." The woman started crying. "He doesn't love my baby."

"Of course he does." Beth patted the woman's shoulder. "Let me get you a Kleenex."

In between sobs, the mother of the bride patted her nose and mouth with the tissue. Her neck tightened as she tried to get herself under control.

Her mascara had not smeared. *Must be waterproof,* I thought.

I tried to imagine my own mother sobbing in the bathroom at my wedding. I couldn't imagine my mother letting me get so far as to marry someone so wrong for me or the family. That image wasn't part of my positive-thinking future.

I sat on my maidservant chair and averted my eyes, which meant I could unobtrusively watch the entire scene in the mirror.

"He's using her."

Beth continued patting the mother's shoulder. "They're in love."

"Did you see them walking down the aisle?"

"They'll be okay."

The mother coughed. "This never would have happened if her father were alive. She would have come back to Illinois long ago. She respected her father. He wouldn't have liked Jonathan."

"Abi will be okay."

"He didn't get to give our baby away." I hoped the swing band drowned out the mother's renewed sobs. The mother was leaning against the wall as if the wall could be her husband, as if the wall could help carry her through the rest of her life.

I stood up and motioned to my seat. The mother sat. Beth continued patting the mother's shoulder and started making a low humming sound. The humming sounded like the flow of the Bitterroot River on a quiet afternoon. I wanted to join in. I wanted the water to flow over the mother and soothe her.

Slowly, as if her heart had room to beat again, the bride's mother quieted. She dabbed her eyes with a fresh Kleenex that I handed to her.

"They'll be okay," the bridesmaid repeated.

"A wedding reverberates forever. Even when it ends," said the mother.

Act Three

"[Martha Graham] said so many interesting things, such as, 'I never think a dancer is alone on stage because there is always the relationship to surrounding space.' My imagination had not run to the possibility of space as a partner. What a comfort that might have been."

—Margot Fonteyn,
Margot Fonteyn: Autobiography

Dancing in the Park

July. Hot. Humid. Upper Manhattan. My black leather dance bag is heavy. We're walking across Dyckman Street, to the edge of Fort Tryon Park, and it looks as if there is very little shade from the trees along either side of the blacktop where we are to perform. The other dancers go on ahead, but I stop at the corner Korean deli at Dyckman and Broadway. Buy two bottles of Gatorade: one, yellowish-green; the other, orange.

Dancing in the park—a ritual during summer in New York City. I'm only making twenty-five dollars a pop for this gig, but it is money and I need it. At least the leg goes high with all the humidity. The hips loosen up, everything is well-oiled. I can't think straight because of heat headaches, but I don't care because my legs are kissing my ears. I've never had great extension, except during a New York summer for a New York minute. The only people to see my legs and their glorious extension are the regular folks who come to the park because they have no air conditioning.

We're a ragtag group of dancers. Some of us take the park performances very seriously. You never know who might be watching! Some of us think the park performances are a riot, something New York to write about to the folks back home.

For me, it's another in a long list of experiences I never dreamed of when I took ballet classes six days a week as a kid. "Just think," Flemming Halby should have said, "someday you'll perform in a New York City park at high noon."

We're dressed in silver colored unitards with chiffon over top. We've decided we're fairies because it provides a reason for gossamer gowns and this dance.

High noon. The show must start on time. After looking for heroin needles, Frank brushed the cement with a broom he brought with him from home and then set up the sound equipment. Sound is just a big old boom box, but we call it sound equipment. That means we are engaged in important and prestigious artistic work. The reality is that we are performing in 100 degree Fahrenheit heat in Upper Manhattan on a Tuesday. Sweat is already showing through our armpits and around our crotches. We're excited because we were listed in the Sunday *Times* calendar.

Frank starts the high-pitched squeaky violin music. It isn't like me, but I never bothered to learn the name of this music or get a copy of it to listen to while riding the subway. I also never learned the actual name of the dance. We just call it "Fairie Nice." I pick a moment where the violin sounds particularly high, and I run across the stage—the cement area with the jungle gym and park benches on one side and the broken water fountain on the other.

I am the beginning, the opening, of the dance. The choreographer Janet Gerson said, "You must feel like the breeze. Be the breeze, Renée."

I am the breeze. I run. I've practiced this a thousand times. The sun is my spotlight, and the trees are my witness, though too far away to provide any shade. I flap my wings—not too hard because I don't want to pass out.

The audience is a collection of people trapped on park benches who never signed up to watch modern dancers in tennis shoes run like sylphs over the blacktop. Their grandkids stop playing, riding their tricycles, carrying beach buckets with no sand, to watch us.

One man calls out, "Fabulous, baby! Do it again." He's wearing white shorts and a white tank top. The tank is so wet from his sweat, you can see his nipples.

I wave at the man, take an unrehearsed spin, flap my arms a little harder, and bow. Everyone claps, including the six onstage. We carry on to some, if not great, acclaim. It's crazy: this performance at high noon on a Tuesday, bringing art to the people.

When the performance is over, I start on my second bottle of Gatorade. The orange one. A dancer must be well hydrated.

Act Four

&

"*A person's body first has to learn to sing in silence. Then you can talk about what you are going to do with a phrase. First and foremost, anticipation. Then, where to rob and steal time: You might delay one part of the phrase, and catch up later. But the extent to which this is done is defined by the character you are portraying. For example, innocence moves in a certain way, and that affects how you use the music. If you are doing a character who is struggling between opposing forces, the movements need more resistance and weight. For example, in Act II of Giselle, Giselle is caught between Myrta, who is trying to pull her into the dark world of the wilis' bitterness, and her own need to save Albrecht from destruction. Mastering a binding quality in the transitions between steps is essential in order to see the struggle, and this becomes a musical challenge as well.*"

—Gelsey Kirkland,
Quoted by Kate Lydon in
Dance Magazine

Daniela Can Fly

When Daniela stepped out her fifth-story window and off the ledge, her toes were pointed. Her arches strong. This was not a test flight. Daniela believed she could fly. She had embodied the Firebird. She was very thin, ninety pounds, and very beautiful, with long, shiny, black hair, which she curled around and around her head into a chignon. The chignon was not a regular ballet bun. It was a twisted mass clipped with two tortoise-shell French barrettes. The pale brown color of the barrettes was the same color as her skin.

Control is always an issue in a dancer's life. Daniela's life was no different. She received a scholarship to the Martha Graham Center and left Buenos Aires for New York City. She controlled the pain of leaving her family. She controlled her desire to return home. Dancers have a necessarily complicated relationship to their body, known as the instrument, and to the sustenance and control of that instrument. As if a flute player needed to clean and oil her flute and live in it all at the same time.

It is modern-dance tradition to work initially from the choreographer's body. It's one of the reasons the idiom of modern dance is so broad and so complicated and yet so fleeting. Modern dance is a collage of vocabulary and technique, and modern dance choreographers are the ultimate collage artists, using not just ballet or other dance vocabulary but any movement: *tendu,* hinge, back fall, walk, run, pretzel, downward yoga dog onto one arm and into a push and a roll. All this comes from the choreographer's body and from somewhere else too. Depending on the unique expression of the artist, the movement looks new. Usually it isn't.

Some modern choreographers have intrinsic body movements that translate more easily to other bodies; Mark Morris, for example, or Doug Varone. Both use their own bodies to start and then borrow at will. Their choreography, their movement, breathes not just because the dancers know how to breathe (and they study yoga to learn that because they don't learn it in a dance class) but also because the movement is not situated only in the choreographer's body. The choreographer translates it to others, shaping and changing his own quirkiness into something more accessible. The dancer isn't dancing for the ego of the leader, although ego is always present, but for palpable and visceral communication.

Daniela already had the ability to create movement with her own body. Later, after she flew, and then after she recovered, she learned to translate it to others. First, Daniela trusted her gut. Second, she imagined the Firebird's mystical vision. She decided to choreograph a piece that was androgynous and feathered.

Daniela envisioned the steps of the mythical bird as light-footed and delicate yet strong. She wanted to evoke a vulnerable, dreamlike aspect because for her Stravinsky's score suggested that birds, metaphorical birds, fly through dream worlds. Regular people on the street might see a Firebird flying overhead, down past windows, but then call the sighting a vision, a dream. Or regular people might even deny seeing the mythical flight. The bird represented beauty and death, in the way that a dying swan evoked those qualities of the romantic age, but the bird represented imagination, too, and the possibility that in the twentieth century metaphor might live as reality. Daniela realized the twenty-first century was too crass for metaphor and certainly too jaded for sentiment, but birds still flew no matter the century.

The Firebird was already a ballet based on a Russian fable. Daniela appropriated the bird and decided to use it in her own choreography. She decided to craft a solo for the Graham Center showcase.

As a young ballet dancer training in Buenos Aires, Daniela had dreamed of dancing the role of Firebird. Those sorts of dreams never die— and if a ballet dancer becomes a modern dancer, they can be appropriated, articulated, and actualized. If a dancer doesn't actualize the dream, it solidifies into bitterness. There is a high probability that former dancers will become bitter birds, scratching through the rest of their lives instead of flying. Yet unrealized dreams also provide the opportunity for ultimate grace, a bowing and surrender of ego, so that one becomes unburdened from ego, finally free from the dream.

Daniela choreographed wild movement straight from her unconscious. She meant her Firebird to be its physical expression. Flight, for her, was not an escape from reality but a manifestation of it. In rehearsal, she rolled from side to side on the floor, slowly and then quickly, her hair loosening and tangling in the process. She started with movement of the bedroom and of the night, crawling along the floor, searching for a moment, a symbol, searching for a means of flight.

For music, Daniela used Stravinsky's *Firebird's* "Lullaby," which occurs in the garden at the end of the ballet. She wanted to focus on the action the bird takes after bringing to life the frozen knights in the garden, envisioning not the knights and their defrosting but what happens to the bird after it helps the humans. She didn't want to focus on Prince Ivan's initial hunt and the bird's appearance. She certainly did not want to stress the Prince's rather predictable love for one of the princesses imprisoned by the evil Kaschei. Prince Ivan smashes the egg to kill the evil Kaschei only because the Firebird showed him what to do. But really, thought Daniela, the Prince only did that to get a woman. Daniela kept imagining that the Firebird was a woman, too, but that wasn't true, she reminded herself. The Firebird was already free—a bird of magnificent plumage with the power to assist humans and then disappear.

Daniela started rehearsing in the upstairs studio at the Graham Center. In the evenings she worked the front desk, checking in students and accepting payment. As part of that work-study job, she had been instructed by the company manager never to give the artistic director any money from the till. She'd been told to say, "I'm sorry, sir, I don't have any cash." It was a ridiculous supposition that a person collecting money for dance classes wouldn't have any money, but it worked. The artistic director just walked away. He was not a dancer. He had been the devoted companion of Martha's last years and as such held the rights to some of her choreography.

It was rumored that Martha had left the artistic director her works because she was so inebriated she didn't know what she was doing. Conversely, it was rumored that Martha knew exactly what she was doing, that she never wanted her works to outlive her and that by leaving the ballets to a nondancer the works would definitely die. For a time, the only way a Graham-trained dancer could perform Graham was by going downtown and joining Richard Move's chorus. Mark Morris said that Move, a drag queen, was more Martha than Martha. Ultimately Graham dancers were so invested in the work—and in a reverse existential way the works were so invested in their bodies—that they refused to let Martha die. She could be channeled cabaret-style by a drag queen, but eventually the dancers needed to perform Martha's dances on a proscenium stage.

After the evening adult Graham class ended, Daniela locked the front doors on 63rd Street. She went upstairs to the second-floor studio. She didn't want to work in the lower studio because that was where Martha had created her ballets. Daniela thought perhaps Martha, looking from her grave, would pay less attention to Daniela's nascent attempts if she used the upstairs studio.

At first Daniela moved without any music. She had rigorous A, B, A components to her Firebird piece already thought out, but she was testing her ideas, working up to moving with Stravinsky.

On the way home to her tenth-floor sublet in the East Village she would visit the Classical section of Tower Records. It helped to calm her down after her choreography sessions. She put on headphones at the listening station and sat on the floor. While listening she realized that most of her rehearsal sessions were failures. Necessary failures. Her first ballet teacher had said that if a dancer didn't fall in class at least once a week, she wasn't trying hard enough. Daniela kept thinking that birds flew in tune to the wind, not music, so when she got home she sat for hours in front of the open window, trying to feel the wind.

"I need to feel flight," Daniela said out loud.

"Well, you're human—not bird!" she answered herself. "Just give the illusion of flight. You don't have to portray the real thing."

℘

Daniela had traveled a long way from Argentina and had a list of sacrifices typical for a dancer: leave family, leave country, forget secondary education, forget any guarantee of a stable income, destroy naïve innocence about the body. Never reclaim any of it. Daniela did not regret the decision to come to Graham. She was becoming a mythical bird.

In the upstairs studio, to warm up, Daniela stood in front of the mirror. She had to imagine how that exotic and fabled descendant of dinosaurs might move. She pledged to discover the movement herself, to be born to the moment, as Martha might have said. She moved her arms like Odette at the end of *Swan Lake*. Daniela thought of the final flight of a swan as a leap into the abyss. Odette leaps into the lake at the end of the ballet after Prince Siegfried has betrayed her. After she has forgiven him. Odette had something to do with being a trapped maiden. But a swan, whether Odette or Odile, Daniela realized while moving her arms, is very different from a Firebird. Daniela gave up trying to move like a swan, or a trapped maiden, and began to move like a Firebird. It was jagged, beautiful movement, rough on the joints, but true to freedom, which is alternately a jolting and graceful journey.

Daniela shook her left leg, a hard shaking right from the hip joint, to loosen her muscles and wake them up. She repeated the action on her right leg. She was so thin, it hardly looked as if there were any muscles in her legs at all, but she imagined she could feel the loosening of the striated muscle tissue. Her bones were becoming aerated, hollow. She began flexing her wrists and moving her fingers, giving the impression of feathers separated by stress, and then she bent and straightened her elbows and moved her arms up to the sky and down to the ground.

She liked the effect. With her fingers moving at the same time, it looked as if she were not human at all, but truly a mythical creature of aerated bone and flight.

"I am Bird," she said aloud, and laughed.

There are two clichés that do not fit the dance world: one, all dancers are anorexic; and two, suicide is a cry for help. Daniela merely embodied her favorite role; she embodied the movement she discovered in the studio. When a Firebird leaps, Daniela realized, it flies.

Daniela tried walking on *relevé,* on the balls of her feet, and pulled a knee up to her chest sharply each time she took a step. The movement was syncopated and fast, and it worked nicely juxtaposed against Stravinsky's "Lullaby" music. She had her entrance for the solo. A step, knee to chest, balance—which was really, really hard—and then both feet down as if the bird was landing on the branch of a golden apple tree. Then she moved her arms up and down with her fingers spread wide, giving the illusion of an underlayer of feathers. Her whole arm became the wing.

At home that night, Daniela sat for an hour in front of the open window. She felt the Firebird within her. She felt the stirrings of flight and a defiance of gravity. She stood up and took a step, sharply drawing her knee to her chest, and then she flexed her wrists and moved her fingers. She was Bird.

Daniela stepped up on the ledge of the open window. She pointed her foot and stepped out the window. She flew.

Act Five

&

"I have formed in my own mind the following reconstruction of the scene."

—Sigmund Freud,
Dora

Letting the Weight Fall Forward

E verything needed a plate. Assorted Danishes—cheese, raspberry, chocolate—all had to be taken out of the paper bag and put on a serving platter. Dr. Hagen's Gouda cheese needed a platter, plus Dr. Hagen needed a separate plate from which to eat the cheese. The paper coffee cups from the Three Brothers Bakery on 86th and Lexington each needed a saucer. What mattered, Dr. Hagen had told me every Sunday for the past year, was that every item had a plate under it, every plate sat on top of a place mat, and every place mat sat on top of a heat protector called a safe mat.

A year ago, when I first started the job with the Freudian psychiatrist, I had not appreciated the table and the need to protect it. Nor had I appreciated how much the safety mats on the table protected the sensitive nature of the doctor herself.

While Dr. Hagen was in the bathroom washing her hands before we ate, I stood up and put a leg on top of the window ledge. I opened one arm to second position, straight out from my shoulder, then reached up to the ceiling, palm up, and stretched my body down over my raised leg. From twenty floors up, it felt as if I were stretching right over the width of Park Avenue. The sensation nauseated me, but also, so far from the concrete earth, I felt as if I were being lifted high over a partner's head and offered to the wind. It could have been the moment in Graham's *Diversion of Angels* when the woman in yellow butterfly-jumps ecstatically into her lover's arms.

The bathroom door opened. I pulled my leg off the windowsill and sat back down at the table. My left hamstring tightened with the quick move-ment. I grabbed underneath my thigh and pressed hard into the muscle as Dr. Hagen walked into the room.

The petite doctor wore a knee-length brown skirt with nylons and a cream-colored silk blouse with a sash collar tied in a loose slipknot. She wore indoor shoes, brown flats with thick soles. She wore medium-sized pearl earrings, which perfectly matched the color of her blouse.

Dr. Hagen always wore earrings and shoes. The same earrings and shoes. I always took off my shoes at the front door. Even when not dancing, I had to feel the floor under the soles of my feet. The soles of my feet had the same approach to the floor as my body had to dance: MUST FEEL FLOOR; GOT . . . TA . . . DANCE.

The dancers I trained with at the Graham Center were a bunch of hyenas circling each other, knowing one person, maybe two, would get into the Company. The rest of us would explain for years to the heathen non-dancer population how we had been successful just because we got so close. (*"Don't you feel bad you were never successful at dance?" asked one of my aunts. We were sitting in my mother's garden in northern Idaho, drink-ing root beer floats. "That's a self-revealing comment," I answered, except I didn't.*) Whatever. There's only one gold medal—except if you perform *Acts of Light.* That was Martha's Halston era, choreographed for her community of devoted dancers, and the costumes, although basic, are all splash and couture. All the unitards are gold colored in that piece.

"Please, please start. You must eat," commanded Dr. Hagen. "You are very thin."

Every Sunday, I thought, and pinched myself hard under the table. If I had been a modern dancer in the fifties, I might not have worried so much about my weight, but as a modern dancer—or as anything female—in the nineties, I worried about my weight constantly. Gone were the days that modern dancers could have massive thighs, that they could be different shapes, that their bodies could be distinguished from ballet bun-heads.

Martha loved trees so much, their growth, their sturdy trunks, but all dancers were expected to be aspens now—not cottonwoods. Most modern dancers didn't even have boobs anymore.

"I didn't want to start eating without you," I said to Dr. Hagen. *As always.*

"How was your performance last night? You must tell me when I can watch you perform."

Dr. Hagen had made a point to learn as much about modern dance as she could from her previous secretaries; like me they had all been students in the professional training program at the Graham Center. Dr. Hagen had attended years of modern dance performances—some, if not most, obscure like the Antipodal Dancers at the SoHo gallery, others, more elegiac and lyrical like the Pearl Lang Dance Theater who used the Danny Kaye Playhouse for her annual season.

Each dancer who worked for Dr. Hagen passed the job onto another, thus keeping a series of dancers employed on Sunday mornings. My POOSSLQ—person-of-opposite-sex-sharing-living-quarters—boyfriend, Chris, found it insufferable that I left him on Sunday mornings to eat breakfast with a Freudian. After all, he had held me up after the Montana Dance Arts Association scholarship auditions for the Graham School. I hadn't been able to walk after the audition. L3 and L4—lumbar vertebrae three and four—radiated pain down both legs. Chris had carried me from the car and into the bathroom, undressed me and himself, and propped me up under the shower. At 6'1" Chris could hold me against his body and off the bottom of the tub while my spine lengthened and popped. Then Chris followed me from Montana to New York City, canceling our lease on a tiny house off Rattlesnake Drive in Missoula, Montana, in the process. Plus, he had yet to finish his undergrad in Russian literature or architecture or computer science—whatever he'd been studying, or planned to study, at that point. What we called "the little house fiasco" cost us over five hundred bucks. It could have been prevented if I had told Chris at the beginning of the summer that there was no way I was coming back to crunchy cowboy country at the end of the summer. In New York, I'd started wearing black, and while a few pastels still entered my wardrobe, I certainly never wore my pink culottes anymore. Chris had tried for a year in Montana to get me to wear earth tones and black, and I'd finally complied all on my own.

Chris said I let Dr. Hagen treat me the way Freud treated Dora. I suspected I let Dr. Hagen treat me in a rather similar manner to Freud's beloved Dora, because Dr. Hagen never answered my questions and Freud had certainly never answered Dora's. Freud had just imposed his will on Dora, his fiction; at the very least, Freud had certainly redirected Dora's questions to parallel his desire. Then he wrote a book about it.

I told Chris I wasn't in psychoanalysis with Dr. Hagen, and she couldn't erase my voice so easily the way Freud had erased Dora's. She couldn't fictionalize me; besides, Dr. Hagen was kinder than that, certainly kinder than Freud had been to Dora. Chris said I didn't have a voice; I was a dancer, and Dr. Hagen had already fictionalized me. He said we needed time together. I said we needed money. Chris said Dr. Hagen thought all I was good for was eating breakfast and filing.

"Then why does she pay me so much?" I asked.

"Who cares?" he said.

"I've given you the wrong idea about her," I said. "She knows all about dance. She loves to watch dance."

"So do I," said Chris. It was true. Chris attended every single one of my performances. He always brought me flowers on opening night. Roses. I always plucked one and gave it back to him. My leading man.

I was working eight jobs, including my bathroom attendant position at South Street Seaport Catering, in addition to dance classes and rehearsal.

Here is the list of eight employers who paid me money to work:

South Street Seaport Catering:	Bathroom Attendant Girl, $10/hr
William Morrow & Company:	Chief Fan Mail Coordinator for Ramona, Ralph S. Mouse, Henry Huggins, Ribsy, and # 1 Fans, $10/hr
Ballet Academy East:	Mommy & Me Teacher, $15/hr
Alvin Ailey American Dance Center:	Creative Movement & Ballet Teacher, $20/hr
Bank Street School of Education:	Creative Movement Teacher, $25/hr
The Stressless Step:	Massage Therapist, $22/hr *(Don't ask.)*
New World Coffee:	Coffee Girl, $7/hr
Dr. Hagen:	*(Current discussion covers this job.)*

Chris was working one job doing programming on the night shift for a temp company called Tiger Information Systems. During slow times, he read and re-read *The Brothers Karamazov*. Chris made more money from one job, even a temp job, than I made from my eight combined. He wanted me to quit all the jobs. He'd support me while I danced full-time, and then I'd spend Sunday mornings with him.

Somehow, I couldn't give up making my own income. I didn't think we could afford it, either. Chris crunched the numbers. His graphs made it look like we could manage. He printed a pie chart and a numbers graph. I was terrible at math, so I didn't believe the numbers. Conversely, I believed numbers were things not to be believed. I was a dancer. I could only count to eight. Over and over again. And I couldn't give up the idea that I had to struggle, to bleed not just in dance, but in my life, too. I was involved in some kind of blue collar struggle where I worked my butt off for ten bucks an hour *(okay, ten to twenty-five bucks an hour, but the higher wage had fewer hours)* and some kind of dancer-bleed-for-hire struggle where I worked my butt off for nothing. Nothing except art and life. *(Later in life, I thought, I can make more money and have a butt and have sex, too.)* Whatever. At least I had a POOSSLQ who loved me enough to rescue me from becoming Dora.

But even though Chris would have gladly given me the money that Dr. Hagen paid me, I still worked every Sunday morning. I walked across Central Park to save subway fare. After work, Chris met me in the park, so we could walk home together. He sat right behind the Metropolitan Museum of Art on a bench with an engraved bronze plaque dedicated to **MME. ENGELS & PHOEBE.**

"Last night," I said to Dr. Hagen, "we did part of Graham's *Acts of Light.* Before the Graham Company audition next week."

I flexed and pointed my feet under the table. I was obsessed with strengthening every muscle in my body. Then I started writing the alphabet with my foot: forward, a, b, c, and all the way through, quickly, and backward, z, y, x, and all the way backward, slowly, because the difficulty I had thinking the alphabet backward was similar to the difficulty counting above eight.

My right ankle still had a little glitch from falling off a staircase while I was pretending to be Madonna dancing to "Like a Prayer." Stupid injury. One of the Polish bars on 7th Street had been playing the song as Chris and I entered, and I missed the last step because I was trying to shove my crotch into Chris's butt. Vodka covered up the pain, and we walked home from 7th on the East Side to 51st on the West Side. The next morning my ankle was the size of a golf ball. I took four naproxen pills twice a day for an entire week to get the swelling down. It should go without saying that I kept dancing and working and walking everywhere to save subway fare. The naproxen worked so well, I shifted back to four pills a night as a regular balm. Sometimes one before class was very helpful, too.

"Did Chris attend last night?" asked Dr. Hagen.

"He comes to everything," I said. "Chris said the dancing looked great. But, you know, even though *Acts of Light* is Martha's ode to her technique, and I practice letting the weight fall forward every class, I felt like I was flailing."

"When I started practicing psychoanalysis in Vienna," Dr. Hagen said, "I often felt as if I were flailing."

There was a crack and a popping sound as my ankle reached l, m, n, o, p.

I knew very little about Dr. Hagen's history. In the living room, an area adjacent to the dining room table with a small couch, an antique coffee table, and two chairs, there was only one personal photograph in a dark wooden frame. It was a colored Polaroid of Dr. Hagen standing in front of the Sigmund Freud Museum during one of her annual summer trips to Vienna. In the photograph, she was wearing pants and smiling. She was smiling so broadly she looked happy.

Claire, the dancer from whom I inherited my job, had respectfully declined to answer any questions and told me emphatically not to ask Dr. Hagen about the past; however, whenever there was an opening, I still tried. "How long did you practice in Vienna?" I asked.

Dr. Hagen carefully moved the cheese platter in front of her, sliced three pieces, and transferred the Gouda slices to the smaller plate. "I have a proposition for you," she said.

"Oh?" I couldn't get used to Dr. Hagen ignoring my questions.

"I need to present a paper," Dr. Hagen continued. "You will write it."

"Me?"

"Claire used to write papers for me."

I shifted in my chair. That left hamstring was starting to cramp again, and my lower back had started to ache. I couldn't sit in one place for long without feeling as if my body was starting to congeal.

"Claire is a Smith graduate," I said. My voice sounded high, the sound coming from my nasal cavity, not my diaphragm. It was shrill, the way I imagined Dora's voice might have sounded when she protested to Freud that she really didn't like the advances of Herr K., that, no, her father's best friend did not arouse her sexually, that, no, she really wasn't in love with him. *(For clarity she might have added, "Nor am I in love with you, Dr. Freud.")*

I think Freud secretly wished Dora was in love with him. Freud was all about control, not hysteria, not psychosexual stages, not even sex, really, just control through erasure of the feminine voice. Freud wanted his friend Herr K. to get it on with his client, Dora, so he could hear all about it. The prurience of the psychoanalyst is not so different from that of the company ballet mistress.

Dr. Hagen fixed her analyst's glare on me. "You are aware English is not my first language. I need someone to write who knows the language."

"I don't know the subject." I wanted to take a big gulp of coffee but could only manage small sips through the plastic opening on the lid.

"I'll tell you."

"You'll dictate the paper to me while I write?"

"No, you'll write the paper. First, we discuss the subject."

Despite early morning sunshine, the sky had turned gray. I hoped the rain would start to pelt against the windows. "Maybe one of your colleagues should come in and work on the paper with you," I said. I was maintaining composure, trying not to be overruled. My ankle popped again at u, t, s, r.

"My colleagues are busy with patients, Renée." As Dr. Hagen spoke, her German accent became stronger. She scratched at her wrist. "And then she scritched herself," I would tell Chris later in the Park.

"The residents are too busy to take the time needed for discussion. Besides, most of the younger people in the profession look more to Prozac than to Freud. That is why I want to present this paper.

"Younger, new members of the profession don't understand how applicable Freud's stages of psychosexual development are to children. I've seen a great number of child patients in consultation. Children always exhibit one of the stages. Often their parents do, too. It's popular nowadays to parent in a highly intrusive manner where the parent becomes a child and the child becomes the little emperor. The child is not allowed to develop sequentially through psychosexual stages. Of course, the child is not to blame for being spoiled."

I suddenly became aware that I was leaning on my elbow and holding my bottom lip between two fingers. I let go of my lip and moved both arms under the table. I had already transitioned from feeling slightly hysterical to feeling bored with the same old discussion of amazing Freud and his amazing discoveries. Hadn't Dora simply said, "No"?

"I don't think I'm the right person for the paper, Dr. Hagen. But it's very generous of you to ask me."

"It isn't generous." Dr. Hagen spoke loudly. "I need you to write the paper."

The orange color of the paper coffee cup clashed with the sedate purple of the china saucer. The coffee cup also had a friendly picture of three brothers waving while you lifted the cup to take sips of burned coffee. Back in Montana, I would have called it trucker coffee. Here in New York, I just called it caffeine.

"I'm not qualified," I said to Dr. Hagen. I spoke very calmly.

Dora must have spoken calmly to Freud. My voice no longer sounded shrill. Dr. Hagen needed help, but this wasn't the way to get it from me. I'd consciously let a Graham teacher control me, beat me down, hit me, but I wouldn't let a non-dancer do it. No way.

Dr. Hagen answered. "I'm the professional; I say whether you're qualified. You studied psychology at university."

Dr. Hagen's voice had had a similar tone once before when I declined an invitation to a lecture called "The Postcolonial Nature of the Id." I'd had a dance rehearsal that night—I'd just started working with the Antipodal Dancers—but in any case, I knew I couldn't sit through such a topic. My body would be stone by the end—not just congealed but solidified into Lot's wife. Did I need to keep reminding Dr. Hagen that Carl Jung was my psychological hero, not Freud?

"Someone still does Freudian analysis?" I had asked when Claire first suggested the job with Dr. Hagen. We had been dressing for the Level IV class, the highest in the Graham School.

"Martha Graham's *Night Journey* is all over the Oedipus Complex," Claire had responded as she pulled on her skin-tight black unitard. Arturo sewed the unitards and sold them, but he'd made this one a little too tight. You could see the lips of Claire's vagina.

"Sure, Jocasta, Oedipus," I answered, defensively, as I twisted my long hair tightly in a bun and clipped it up with two barrettes.

"Noguchi's sets seem more primeval than Freudian, though," another dancer said.

"Greek. Brutal," said Amanda, in her British accent. Even before the audition and call backs, she had been made an apprentice with the Company.

"Dr. Hagen pays very well," Claire had said as we walked down the stairs and entered the large studio for class. I pulled off my faded pink sweatpants, which had a patched hole in the leg. I had always been wary of dancers who were nice. Usually dancers were competitive, not nice.

Without looking at Dr. Hagen, I took a deep breath. In a purposefully measured tone I said, "I did study psychology at the University of Montana, but as I told you, I put my degree on hold so that I could come to Graham when they gave me the scholarship. I haven't finished my degree."

"There's no need to be defensive. You've been with me a year, Renée. That is long enough to help me write a paper on Freud." Dr. Hagen folded her fingers together and rested them on the table. Her fingernails were short and unpolished. She could listen to people's problems and write prescriptive solutions, which in Freud's tradition privileged the doctor's interpretations over the patient's. Dr. Hagen preferred not to engage in discussions. She was not adept at compromise. "I will pay you $45 per hour for the time we spend on the paper and for the time you spend writing at home on your computer."

"I don't have a computer." It was a lie; although, technically true because the new Gateway was Chris's purchase, not mine.

"You'll go to Kinko's. I will instruct you on what to say. You will put it into the proper words."

Last week, I had almost quit when Dr. Hagen leaned over my shoulder. "Are you filling in the correct numbers?" Dr. Hagen had asked directly into my ear. Her breath didn't smell badly, sort of sour-sweet, but the closeness made me dreadfully uncomfortable. I felt as if I'd done everything wrong—not only by filling in the wrong numbers in the wrong boxes, which I hadn't—I'd been very careful—but also for my entire life. I needed analysis if only to become someone else. Someone who wrote numbers in boxes without protest, with gratitude. But Dr. Hagen asked the same question every time I filled out the insurance forms.

"I'm filling in the code for generalized anxiety disorder: 300.02," I said. In Dr. Hagen's practice, everyone had the same disorder, so each patient was assigned the same number.

"Are those the correct numbers?" the doctor had repeated.

My line was supposed to be, simply, "Yes," but last week I had said, "Maybe we should find some new numbers for you." It had slipped out, unprotected and hurtful.

While I walked to work on Sunday mornings, I lectured myself sternly: Where else would I find a job that paid $35 an hour to eat breakfast, sort mail, look at the Manhattan skyline, and fill out insurance forms with the number 300.02, which really was the number five if added together? Even if Chris wanted me at home Sunday mornings, the money really was too good to give up. Seventy bucks for two hours.

"Let me sort through this week's mail and double-check the insurance forms, and I'll think about writing the paper for you," I said.

"I have to submit a proposal Wednesday in order to be included in the next Freud conference. We write the proposal today. I'll get the notepad."

Dr. Hagen got up from the table and walked quickly down the hall and into her consulting room. Her soft-soled shoes squeaked on the parquet. The consulting room for patients was in the same apartment where she lived; however, I did all the administrative work at the black mahogany dining room table with carved lions inlaid on each leg.

I began clearing dishes off the table. It took several trips back and forth to the small walk-in kitchen to remove all the plates and heat protectors. Then I covered one end of the table with a heavy silver drop cloth to protect the wood.

I had just finished sorting the mail when Dr. Hagen reemerged from her consulting room with two yellow legal-sized pads of paper. She sat down at the table and handed me one of the notepads.

"Let's begin," said Dr. Hagen, her accent subdued.

"I could ask Claire to do the paper with you," I suggested. "She knows your style."

"If I wanted Claire, I would have asked Claire. In any case, she's auditioning for the Graham Company this week. She's too busy."

"Me, too." I covered the middle of my chest with my palm as if that gesture alone were enough to get me in the Company and to protect me from being manipulated by Dr. Hagen. Even if I agreed with Dr. Hagen about neurotic contemporary parenting philosophies, I sure hadn't moved to New York City to spend my time helping a psychiatrist write a paper about Freud. Not in good conscience. Not in Dora's name.

"Me, too, what?" Dr. Hagen's voice sounded sharp and staccato. The sound reminded me of the notes demanding three back falls in quick succession from the Furies in Graham's *Clytemnestra,* which I had studied in repertory class.

"I'm auditioning for the Graham Company, too."

"Let's begin. When new members of my profession understand the pregenital phase, they can help children control their anxiety."

"That's our topic?"

"Write it down. First, we'll highlight and discuss the oral and anal stages so professionals can use the information in their practice. Then we direct professionals to explain the stages to parents."

(Oral stage: excitation related to the lips of the mouth. Anal stage: excitation related to the anal mucous membrane.)

Dr. Hagen continued. "Once parents accept that these stages exist, then everyone can understand that childhood anxieties relate directly to Freud's oral and anal stages. But, of course the psychoanalytical trick is to get the patient unstuck."

"I thought the point of psychoanalysis was the understanding of one-self. If so, why use tricks?" I put down the pen. Certainly tricks must lead to more shame and sexuality blah, blah, blah, I thought. I was glad my POOSSLQ and I didn't have any problems in that area other than my never wanting to do it because I was so physically tired, which is a problem, I guess, but whatever. It isn't as if we never had sex—at least, once a month.

(Dear Dr. Freud: Sex isn't everything. Sincerely, Dora.)

"You see, Renée, you understand quite nicely."

I held my stomach muscles tight, readying the muscles of my abdomen for the ever-present contraction, the hallmark of Graham's movement. The strange, organic, and powerful beauty of Graham dancers comes from years of training in how to use the back muscles and pelvis in coordination with the breath not simply to create movement, but to explore emotion through physical action. Graham motion is emotion physically realized.

By engaging the muscles in my back, I pulled my scapula down and into the upper portion of my lower back, using the technique Graham classes taught from the very first floor exercises—even the ridiculous opening bounces for sixteen counts. Well, two eights. The muscular action and combined inhale of breath made my back straighten and my chest rise.

If movement happens from the pelvis and because of breath, then I am breathing and moving myself out the door right now, I thought.

Two years ago when I moved from Montana and started at the Graham School, I had found it hard—impossible—to breathe while doing all these actions. Now—sitting at Dr. Hagen's table—those muscular actions gave me a sense of inner power, and quite suddenly, the ability to stand up for myself. *Go, Dora,* I thought.

"Dr. Hagen, I can't help you with the paper," I said.

"You'll never be hired as a dancer unless you follow orders," retorted Dr. Hagen.

"You aren't hiring me to dance. You hired me for administrative work, which I will continue to do. But I can't write your paper this week."

"I'm firing you."

Doesn't Freud seem out of date, I wanted to plead, *with what we've learned about the subconscious from Jung?* Instead, I walked to the door and put on my shoes. Dora did the same thing. Well, not quite. She didn't walk out of analysis, but she never finished it either. No wonder Dora bothered Freud so much. He couldn't control her.

"Claire will come help me," said Dr. Hagen.

"Yes, she will," I said. *And I'll get in the Graham Company.* It was more powerful not to say my wish out loud. It was more powerful to hold it in my body.

As I had practiced countless times in Graham class, I let my weight fall forward, caught myself on a straight supporting leg, and using the stately, sometimes stiff Graham walk, proceeded out the door.

Once in the hall, I turned. Dr. Hagen stood in the doorway. She looked small, framed in the rectangle of the door, and vulnerable. Her face was drawn into a pinched frown.

"Please come back on Sunday mornings," said Dr. Hagen.

I stepped my legs apart the way the chorus woman takes her place on Noguchi's rock in *Cave of the Heart.* Immovable in conviction yet still moving.

"I'll let you know," I said. My voice sounded harsher than necessary, but at least it didn't sound shrill.

"If you get in the Company, I'll buy an orchestra seat to watch you perform," said Dr. Hagen. She closed the door.

I cupped my palm into a Martha hand. The cupped hand, made as if you were to hold water in the palm, shows the vulnerable tendons connecting the forearm to the hand in the same way a tilted head shows the vulnerable sternocleidomastoid muscle where a wolf *(or a hyena)* can bite through to the carotid artery and brachial plexus.

Like the chorus woman in *Cave of the Heart* calling all gods, I shook my cupped palm forward and back over my open mouth. I waited for the elevator.

Act Six

"*The person drawn to dance as a profession . . . thinks with [her] muscles; delights in expression with body, not words; finds analysis painful and boring; and is a creature of physical ebullience.*"

—Doris Humphrey,
The Art of Making Dances

Living Figure

At the Martha Graham Center for Contemporary Dance, we called Mara a goddess, partly because she had bodacious breasts, partly because she always had a new lover, partly because she was from Argentina, but mostly because we adored her. Our boyfriends started it.

Sandra's boyfriend, soon-to-be husband, said "Mara? Oh." His throat caught, and you knew his groin was in his stomach, which was remarkable because Mike was six foot five and had long legs. "She's a goddess."

Even my boyfriend, Chris, said to me, "Mara? Woman." Emphasis on the "wo" part, a woman made for man.

The men always said it with an upswing at the end, as if they wanted their desire to be okay with us. Yes. It was.

Mara was an "athlete of the gods," as Martha Graham would say, and she had a lot of sex. She was unencumbered by fidelity. When Mara did jumps in Graham class, after the floor exercises and center work, her breasts bounced with her. The American girls, including me, were so impressed with the sight of freely moving breasts, full, voluptuous breasts, slightly bound by a bra but basically the two moving separately and uniquely and beautifully, that we realized Mara's fleshy movement underscored the flesh missing from our own bodies.

Those of us with breasts, including me, lashed our mounds down with ace bandage tape or shoved them into sports bras to prevent any bounce. My sports bra meant that I had a flat mound across my chest, a shelf of breast, the two mashed together in one full baguette of boob. I never wanted my breasts to bounce or to move at all. It was because an old ballet teacher, seeing me after I entered puberty, said, "Oh my God, what happened to you?" And then she laughed. Cackled. *I'm becoming a woman,* I had thought to myself at the age of fifteen. The thought probably saved me.

Mara always encouraged me to wear a Brazilian bra. "Let them be free," she'd say. "They're beautiful. Part of your body. Don't strap them down."

I wanted to believe Mara. I wanted to trust her. But except for Mara, we were supposed to be breast-free, a physical type closer to that of young boys. The women were supposed to have flat chests and no meat, and the men were supposed to be men, gay or not. I knew one male dancer who rearranged his penis and testicles so they looked bigger—a mound between his legs. Onstage Baryshnikov looked like he had a mound, but I couldn't imagine Misha rearranging his parts in his dance belt. That seemed antithetical to having *cojones* or whatever the word for balls is in Russian.

Mara wore skimpy bras and low-cut unitards. She had slim hips, so the upper portion of her body naturally drew the eye to it. One could see her cleavage, and realize the hunger for physicality that had some flesh to it. Not dough, mind you, but seductive, gorgeous flesh moving across a dance studio. Mara was more gorgeous, more heavenly, and more available than the rest of us. She didn't need to be the Sugar Plum Fairy. She just needed a green card.

Even though I knew Mara lived with Luis, I also knew she had many lovers. Mara was not shy. She told me all about her affairs. She mentioned them off-handedly as if everyone had a lover. I had thought desire was something to be thwarted or at least contained.

Mara and I became friends when a fearless choreographer named Andrea Harris, who also studied at Graham, asked us to be in the same piece for a performance at the Cunningham Studio in Westbeth. Even though I'd performed in student showcases at the Martha Graham studios, I considered Andrea's piece *Anomie* the first time I performed in New York City. I thought *Anomie* suggested that desire makes everything go haywire.

The trio had an intruder, in the form of a trench coat streaker, who ran through the middle of the piece, surprising the three dancers. The streaker made me very excited, even though he flashed the audience and not us, because it was Ian Butler, who was fabulously gorgeous with an English accent to boot. I dreamed of dancing with him, especially after I saw him perform at City Center as one of the attendants in Graham's *Rite of Spring*. And I mean I dreamed of dancing with him—not sleeping with him. There is a difference.

The streaker section in Andrea's dance began with me, Mara, and Kristi standing in a diagonal line. I was the farthest downstage, Mara was in the middle, and Kristi was upstage. We wore black tights and leotards and funky multi-colored vests. Kristi was flat-chested, but Mara and I popped all the buttons on our vests and had to sew them shut. I strapped my breasts into my Wonder-Woman-from-the-Moon bra, which was really a sports bra with wide straps, four hooks, and underwire.

The three of us stood parallel. We made fists and jammed them together in a truncated version of scissors, paper, rock, which only involved the movement of rock—no scissors and no paper. After we pounded our fists together three times, we opened our feet into three consecutive positions, starting from parallel and opening to second parallel and then to a wide second, which twisted into a spiral to the floor and back up again.

After rising from the floor, we had to jump straight up three times quickly, pulling our knees high to our chests and jumping as high as possible. Usually I hit my nose with my knees and gave myself a little nose bruise. Out of the corner of my eye, I saw Mara's bust heaving up and down.

Whether in rehearsal or performance, Mara had a way of moving that seemed verdant, as if she were blooming. She infused each movement of every dance with connectivity. Every single movement looked as if the motions were ivy crawling out from and back to each part of her body. Mara hadn't always moved this way. In the beginning, she'd looked jerky, having difficulty actively connecting steps so that there was a continuous rooted sensation. It was partly the transition from Flamenco to modern.

Mara talked constantly about the music of Argentinean-born contemporary composer Osvaldo Golijov. His extraordinary music opened my mind to what music might be in the same way that Mara opened my mind to differing expressions of love. Or, more specifically, she opened my mind to what breasts might be. I went to Macy's and bought a Vanity Fair purple-maroon lacy bra with matching thong, and I showed them to Mara in the dressing room. On my body.

"Scandalous," she said. "You're learning."

Mara desperately wanted to choreograph a piece using Golijov's music, which we talked about in our underwear in the dressing room—well, in our thongs—our breasts not yet clothed for the outside world. Mara showed me the results of her Brazilian wax job and how she didn't have any pubic hair showing the way I did. Mara said she had no subject other than desire to choreograph. She needed something more specific, she said, such as the breaking of a heart because of the thrust of the wind.

"Come home with me to Idaho," I said. "I'll show you the wind."

Her original teacher in Argentina had studied at the Graham School in the sixties, so she added a few Graham classes, putting a heavy emphasis on the technique's animal components. At the end of each class she let the girls pretend to be cougars stalking or gazelles leaping or bison stampeding across the diagonal. The girls, and an occasional boy, loved to take off their flamenco shoes and dance barefoot.

Mara had come to New York City to dance for The Joffrey. She had seen The Joffrey perform Kurt Jooss's famous anti-war ballet, *The Green Table,* and promised herself that someday she'd move to New York City to dance with them. By the time she was old enough, The Joffrey had relocated to Chicago. But like Hubbard Street Dance Chicago, Joffrey often auditioned in New York.

Mara auditioned at the first opportunity. Number 63. After the second cut, the Ballet Mistress, a small flaming guy who later found his home with *Les Ballets Trockadero de Monte Carlo*, pulled her to side. "Darling, you have gorgeous breasts, but you don't have enough ballet training for this company."

Mara told me he enunciated and puckered his lips so that every word sounded as if it ended with a kiss. Mara puckered her own bright red and fulsome lips and made a kissing sound when she mimicked him. *Starlet,* I thought, when she did it. Mara had thought of The Joffrey as a fusion company and did not even realize that she needed to do pointe work to be hired. Unlike me, she had never put on a pair of pointe shoes.

After she was cut from the audition for her dream job with The Joffrey, Mara phoned home. "Immigration wanted to export me back to Argentina," she told me. "My visa was ready to expire, and I had nowhere to go."

Mara's teacher arranged for her to enroll in the visa program at the Martha Graham Center. For some reason, Mara had just assumed The Joffrey would take her. It was a benefit of belief. When they didn't, she took the next step. It was a benefit of character. She was adept at change, at moving forward in her life, except, it turned out, when it came to Luis.

Mara had never had little girl ballerina dreams, so she wasn't all hung up on dying Odette or crazy Giselle or the tasty Sugar Plum Queen. Unlike me. At Pacific Northwest Ballet, when I was a Russian Attendant Girl for Act II of *Swan Lake,* I stood in the wings and cried as Siegfried mistook Odile for Odette. *No,* I had said under my breath, *she's not the one. Don't confuse the white swan with the black.*

Mara wasn't all hung up on the American fantasy of a white knight on a horse who rescues his princess. She didn't need to do a fish dive into a savior's arms. Besides, Luis wasn't white and he wasn't tall and he didn't wear armor. And he certainly didn't own a horse. Mara met Luis at Pampa, the Argentinean steakhouse on Amsterdam Avenue where she worked as a waitress. Mara needed a place to live. Luis was convenient. And he was an American citizen.

Mara told me she'd already failed at her first dream of dancing with The Joffrey, so she would tackle her second, lesser dream of dancing for Graham. Mara noticed that the dancers who were practical and even a little dull seemed to have better success at sticking it out in the environs of Martha Graham's shadow.

Luis touched Mara constantly, and when we all had dinner together he couldn't keep his hands off her. Luis was thin and lean and short. Olive-toned skin. Black hair. Mara said she thought her mother would like his black hair. She left it unsaid that her mother wouldn't like anything else about him.

Luis explained to me that he understood he was a trust-fund Bohemian, who did not need to buy into the cultural paradigm of marriage and fidelity in order to offer Mara American citizenship through marriage. Romantic love, which often led to marriage, was a fantasy—something peculiarly American, something unworthy of passion, something that destroyed the economic realities of marriage. Marriage was a middle-class structure, founded on a false promise of love.

Mara was twenty-three, and Luis was thirty-five. Mara had started planning for her green card immediately after they met.

Yet Mara continued sleeping with other men. She thought Luis understood this fact even though they never talked about it. They never discussed monogamy or the limits of acceptable sexual encounters the way an American couple would discuss what could or could not happen outside their relationship—as if desire can be controlled and regulated and then, under lock and key, offered as a sign of allegiance.

Mara told me there were mornings, especially in winter, when Luis massaged Mara's thighs. She used her thighs too much, she said, especially for extension, instead of her adductors on the inside of her legs. Her muscles were getting bulky instead of streamlined; that was part of the reason she often woke in the middle of the night with leg cramps. She'd yell and then lose her breath. Luis leaned over, pulled back the covers, and actively compressed the tops of her thighs with the heels of his hands.

Mara drank Gatorade even during class to try and prevent the cramps. "It's an awful American sugar drink that seems just like America," she whispered to me during the Level IV class. "It's superficial and sugary sweet in a fake way."

Mara's chiropractor suggested she eat half a cup of cottage cheese with a banana every day. Dr. Peter was also my chiropractor and suggested the same thing to me. He'd danced for Jiří Kylián with Nederlands Dans Theater and took umbrage at those choreographers who didn't equally distribute the stress on the right and the left side of the body. He took umbrage at Martha Graham's work, and with reason. He felt the swollen erector spinae muscles on our backs. Dr. Peter said calcium wasn't enough—we needed a combination of calcium and magnesium and potassium. We went to him as religiously as we went to our Graham classes. Every day.

Mara and I both thought New York was tough and full of hardened dreams and rough hearts and accents that were difficult to understand. Luis spoke Spanish with Mara; she said she felt more at home in his apartment in the 10027 area code than anywhere else in the city. There was a bodega a few blocks away, and she bought fresh fruit there and mixed greens for their salads and an herbal potion to keep off her weight. The herbal potion was one of the few things she didn't like to discuss.

When I visited one early fall Saturday, she told me she was planning on leaving Luis, but she couldn't quite figure out her finances. She sliced the corn off the cob and added it to fresh tomatoes, all of which she simmered briefly on the stove. She added garbanzo beans and paprika and served the medley over couscous. We had salad after the main meal and then espresso.

Mara described how after Luis massaged away her leg cramps, he turned her over and entered her from behind. Mara didn't move because she didn't want her hamstrings to cramp as a reaction against the relaxed quads, but Luis didn't mind. I think he loved feeling power over her, feeling her stillness and his expanse, holding down her wrists as he hummed a few piano chords from his new symphony. Mara told me she kept thinking of Luis's brother and how he had surely had sex by entering men from behind. She thought Luis was trying to emulate his brother. Somehow, I think Mara imagined herself as the lifeline between them. It may be what I recall or it may be hearsay, but I remember that Jorge, Luis's brother, had died during the early days of AIDS when the CDC scientists knew what was going on and politicians refused to say, "Use a condom."

This is the story I made up about Mara, Jorge, and Luis:

Luis had grown up in eastern Brooklyn and at eighteen moved into Manhattan to live with his older brother. The brothers spoke Spanish with Argentinean accents because their mother had come from that country. Luis's older brother Jorge was a painter and a self-identified homosexual. That was important because Jorge's identity politics were part of his art politics. The political part of his art, when described, made people suspicious of his skill as an artist, but Jorge was very good. Jorge was a curious man and understood that life was meant to be lived—not endured.

Jorge supported Luis financially while Luis attended the Manhattan School of Music and composed unintelligible avant-garde symphonic works for which there was no need and no acclaim. As opposed to Luis and his symphonic compositions, Jorge actually made his living from selling his art. In the early eighties, Jorge had been identified by "New York Magazine" as one of ten upcoming visual artists to watch, so he'd subsequently been represented by a gallery and sold work to European and American collectors. Jorge's art was considered avant-garde, like his brother's music, but unlike his brother's music, it was good.

I think Luis told me Jorge could never figure out why his work was marketed as cutting edge, but he didn't quarrel with his sales and simply continued painting. Jorge used egg tempera on wooden triptych frames. He was a city queer, but he loved the color green. His subjects were the flowers and plants of New York juxtaposed against the detritus and garbage of the city. He painted the lilac walk at the top of Sheep's Meadow with plastic bottles at the base of the plants, the clipped hedges at Tavern on the Green with plastic bags hanging off the gorilla's arms or the elephant's trunk. In Jorge's work, the trees in front of the Metropolitan Museum of Art had huge green dumpsters under them, and the community gardens in the East Village were filled with rats nibbling green carrot tops.

By the time Mara met Luis, Luis was living in what had once been Jorge's and Luis's apartment together, and he had become financially solvent. He'd inherited his brother's estate, if it could be called that, when Jorge died in 1990. Most of his brother's paintings were owned by private collectors, but there were two triptychs that Luis still owned. One he kept in the bathroom and the other in an alcove room between the living room and bedroom. I thought I first saw them when Mara invited me over for lunch one day after Andrea Harris's performances at Cunningham.

Although they worried about the steam from the shower affecting the tempera, Mara and Luis never moved the painting from the bathroom because Jorge had hung it there. Not moving what the dead have last touched is a superstitious practice followed by the living particularly if the deceased was young when he left this world.

Uncharacteristically for Jorge's work, the subject of "Composer Piano," the painting in the bathroom, was of a man—Luis, the brother—playing the piano with a woman dancer standing at the piano. Luis and Mara considered it prophetic, even though Jorge had never known Mara and even though Luis and Mara didn't believe they were in love. There were piano strings on the side panels of the triptych, against a soft yellow backdrop, as if the composer only needed strings to create.

When I saw it, or thought I saw it, I recall thinking the painting suggested the piano was unnecessary to the act of musical creation. Even the dancer standing next to the painting was unnecessary. And yet the painter, Jorge, sat the composer, his brother Luis, at a grand piano and actively placed a hat on his head, which made it hard to know if he was looking at the piano keys or the woman. In the painting the composer's fingers are so big they spilled over into the left side panel, becoming part of the painted strings of that panel. The strings on the right panel were real: Luis's brother had strung them through the wood, and they even made a little dissonant sound if played.

Both Luis and Mara showed me how to open and shut the panels. They said they closed off the creative work or opened it by opening or closing a panel, depending on the day. It was okay to open and close the triptych door panels, but it was not okay to move the painting. After Mara told me it was okay to touch the panel doors, I opened the right panel, listening to the creaking sound as I did so, and plucked the piano strings, which made an off-key dissonant sound.

The other, larger triptych was from Jorge's later work, in 1989, the year before he died. The larger triptych hung in the room between the kitchen and the bedroom, which was properly called a piano room. A piano room suggested too much artistic pressure, however, so Mara referred to it as "a little room" even though the room was quite large.

Luis had his grand piano and computer and electronic music equipment in there. The panels of the triptych were lopsided and the hinges hung slightly askew, as if Luis's brother had known his life was to be cut short, as if he weren't sure why he had even lived. He had lived very briefly, after all, in the modern scheme of things, only to die. Jorge named it "Living Figure Triptych" with a nod to Henry Moore, his favorite sculptor, although Jorge's work was neither as luscious nor as sensuous as Moore's.

All Jorge's painting titles had to end with the word "triptych" because they were all triptychs. Jorge had tried to get away from the triad for a while, but the effort hadn't worked artistically, politically, or personally. In "Living Figure Triptych," the middle panel was five feet high.

The left, feminine panel was only a foot high. The right, masculine panel was three feet high, except it hung off its hinge and below the entire rest of the structure. It was impossible to shut the doors on the panel or to shut out the subject, which, appropriately, was death. It was a blue figure, reminiscent of Picasso's blue and bony guitar player, but the figure wasn't yet physically emaciated as was Picasso's old man. Picasso's old blue man had lived, perhaps not a good life, but at least a long life. Jorge's figure was emaciated spiritually, though, and it was obvious because the pieces of a cross were pasted collage-like around his neck.

The figure looked straight out at you, shaking his hands, his eyes sunken, his hair stringy and oily. Luis told me he didn't remember that his brother had been angry at the end, or that his hair was oily. He had had beautiful, wavy brown hair. Luis had told Mara that his brother Jorge took care of the details of his death, carefully, that he smiled a lot, and that he said he felt relieved because he knew Luis would always be taken care of financially. For a while Jorge's last lover looked in on Jorge while he died, helping out Luis with the care of his brother, but then he stopped. Jorge's last lover failed at compassion, in the way people do, when the necessary object of their compassion is too similar to the product of their pain.

Whether my story about Jorge is real or not, there seemed to be a hole inside Luis that he didn't know about. Mara told me it hadn't been hard for Luis to offer to marry her so she could obtain her green card and stay in the United States. She said that had to account for some kind of love, some lack of hole. The simple reality might be that Mara kept Jorge alive for Luis. That was her love. But she needed to look elsewhere for her front-facing pleasure.

Mara's first affair was with a businessman in the legal office where she had signed up to do a few days of translation work. The firm had a deal with a bank in Buenos Aires and needed a Spanish translator to assist. Mara got the job through a friend of a friend, a network of performers from other countries who did translation work during the down time from their main artistic careers. The pay was all cash, all under the table, and if any of the lawyers had been appointed to government positions they wouldn't have been able to accept because of the illegality of all the transactions.

Mara's second affair was with her Gyrotonics instructor, a tall blonde Swede. He had come to New York to learn how to use the new machines. Gyrotonics is a combination of exercises using machines designed by a man named Juliu Horvath. It streamlines the muscles and is very popular with dancers because of its resistance training. Mara and her instructor worked late into the night at the studio and used the table of the machine as a bed after their practice sessions. They communicated through touch, and he never entered her from behind.

Then Mara began an on-and-off affair with a dancer. A German. They kept meeting at auditions and sleeping with each other afterward, if they were in the same cut. Alex was a Broadway gypsy dancer who already performed in musicals, but his love was modern, so Mara met him at Bill T. Jones, Bebe Miller, Petronio, and David Dorfman auditions. Mara and Alex directed their love-making to the quality of the preceding audition—funky for Bill T., flowing and lyric for Bebe, fast for Petronio, and all upside down for Dorfman. Her cramps subsided when she began dancing upside down, or maybe she saw her reality more clearly and as a consequence had less muscle tension.

Mara was my inspiration when I expressed my desire for an installation artist named Arthur who provided our tech support, lighting and music, and general setup at the Antipodal Gallery performances. The affair didn't work out very well for me, or at least not as well as I imagined Mara's affairs worked out for her.

My role model as an aspiring ballerina, before I changed to modern dance, had been the Sugar Plum Fairy, and she's not the sort of fairy to have affairs. I am very good at carrying guilt for passion expressed or simply imagined. The Sugar Plum doesn't exactly express passion so much as she expresses ethereal goodness. My guilt has something to do with wanting to do everything right, and passion, I think, makes everything go wrong. Unless it is passion for dance. Then the blood falls in all the right places. Maybe my boyfriend Chris and I should have danced together, but he said he liked to watch me dance with others, he didn't want to move, his feet were lead. "Basketball is the same as ballet," he used to say. "It's a dance, too."

I reprimanded myself in a fragment: *As if qualitative and quantitative disagreements about sports and dance can be used as an excuse for an affair.*

When Arthur and I bent over the wooden floor together in the Antipodal Gallery, Arthur reached out and gently lifted my hair away from my face. I rarely wore my hair loose—it was always clipped back or in a ponytail—but if I was really attracted to a man, I released my hair. I thought Arthur's loping long-legged body was incredibly cute, in a gangly way, so I had not yet clipped my hair back for our tech rehearsal. I wanted him to notice me. Before entering the gallery, I had taken out my clip and scrunched up my hair with my hands. I wanted to look like a free spirit, one unencumbered by protocol and fully proficient in the flirtatious arts. A contemporary Isadora with flowing hair but an abdomen shaped and sculpted by Graham's technique. I had always told my brothers, who gave me a bad time about how much I liked to flirt, that I was the best kind of flirter because I also put out. Of course, those adolescent conversations were a long time ago, and I had made those comments long before I met Chris.

In reality, I was terrified that I would cheat on Chris. He had told me that was the one thing he could not abide, and he would leave me in a second if I did it. I thought of love and commitment as a ballet move, as something to be perfected and then performed, as if love could be held in a still shape, in a position like a *passé*. But a *passé* forms the foundation for a *pirouette,* and Chris and I were definitely no longer turning together.

Arthur let his hand linger on my back, and I thought of my foot on Chris's leg at night. At night, Chris didn't want me to hold him while we slept. But I needed to feel him, so he let me reach out my right foot and touch his leg. My lonesome foot a shallow and limited expression of sexual desire.

I looked at Arthur, and he looked back as if he understood all about that right foot of mine, as if he wanted to hold back my hair so that he might better see my eyes.

I wanted to say, I feel for you, but instead I said, "Are those red long underwear you're wearing?"

He said, "It's a Union Jack suit. All cotton, all buttons, but good underneath for winter."

"Maybe I could undo those buttons?" I asked.

"As long as you undo them slowly," he answered.

We continued taping down the electrical wire for the overhead stage lights—a truncated form of stage lights with minor gels, but one that worked very well for the main room of the gallery. Arthur used the duct tape, and I held the wire down to the floor, pressing the tape down as he dispensed it from the roll. Instead of kneeling, I stood and bent over my legs, taking a step as we moved slowly toward the sound and lighting board at the back of the room.

When I went to Arthur's apartment in Alphabet City, we sat down on his bed and held hands. Chris and I held hands all the time, and it was intimate in a long-standing way, but this feeling with Arthur was beyond intimacy. It was the intimacy of sexual desire, electric yet still and quiet at the same time. Arthur reached over and brought my head into his chest, and I started kissing him and taking off his long-sleeved T-shirt. Underneath was his red-cotton Union Jack suit.

My hands were shaking, and I didn't even mind because I wanted him to see me shake. I wanted him to see my fragility, as if this body of muscles, this inadequate body that ached from too much dance, ached now because I suffered from desire, as if desire would eat me alive were I to allow a yearning for human flesh to replace my craving for movement.

"Feel me," I said, inadequately.

Arthur took my whole body into his lap and rocked me back and forth. He was very tall and very lean and his vertebrae protruded slightly from his back. He was both skeletal and muscular and there was something in his hands and arms that made me want to stay as small and little as possible.

"I feel you," he said.

And we didn't even laugh that the sentiment was stupid or romantic or needy. I thought my epithelial tissue might crack suddenly and snakes would emerge because I had suppressed desire for so long.

For a while, I had turned off the night because the day was physically so rigorous. I didn't care that there were two parallel males in the room—one real, existing, Arthur, and the other, hovering, Chris. While I kissed Arthur, I was kissing Chris. Arthur took his hands and took off my shirt. He left my bra on and placed both his palms on my stomach. I was lying on my back, figuring out whether I could lie still and wait or whether I should touch Arthur even though I felt I were not only touching him but also touching Chris.

When Arthur entered me, I imagined Chris, frantic, trying to figure out why I hadn't yet come home at 3 a.m. when I had another performance the next day. The wind had entered us, and it needed to pass through. Next time, he took off my bra. He let my mounds become breasts.

Surely Chris knew right away that I had acquiesced to desire, that I had submitted to betrayal because of my own selfish need, and there was no possible way to stop. Except with tears. Which came.

As I lay my head in Arthur's lap and looked up, he took my lower lip between his two fingers and pulled and squeezed gently, moving slowly along the whole lip. Suddenly there was nothing else except for what existed between his fingers and in his sight. His reflection back to me was not like the dance studio mirror, unforgiving and harsh, but soft, as if he saw all of me and needed no change. I felt whole in Arthur's sight. This moment. These lips. This twin-sized bed with a popcorn quilt bedspread. Two bodies.

Perhaps any kind of betrayal helps you move forward in a life, whether the failing is romantic and personal or passionate and professional. I think

Mara understood that the expression of romance and of passion is neither a commitment to, nor a failure of, love. But for me, my betrayal felt so immense that soon after leaving Martha's House of Pelvic Truth, I also had to leave Chris.

Act Seven

֍

"There are no famous dances about the death of a noble horse or 'The Dying Dog.'"

—Doris Humphrey,
The Art of Making Dances

Audition # 99

After I got cut from the Graham Company audition and finished my Graham Training Certificate, I left Martha's House of Pelvic Truth and actively started auditioning for all sorts of companies. I wanted the practice, and an audition was an easy way to check out a choreographer's movement without committing to classes in that style of technique.

In order to get into a company, or work with a certain choreographer, usually you took class at a studio where the choreographer taught. You hoped someone noticed and asked you to dance with them. Sometimes, I was really bold, and I told certain choreographers I wanted to dance for them. Kevin Wynn was one of those choreographers, but he didn't take me into his pick-up group until I'd taken class from him for two years, which included charging the $1,000 fee for his workshop at the Bates Dance Festival on my credit card. That price included a work-study discount.

Mary Anthony asked me to perform in her gala at the Danny Kaye Playhouse because I started taking classes at her studio at Kun-Yang Lin's urging. Some of the downtown choreographer's classes were too slow during the warm-up, and I really liked taking classes from Mary, because even though it was hard, the technique had similarities to Graham. Mary's class was old-school modern dance, which felt surprisingly good. There were hinges and falls, and I loved the section of class that included Sufi turns. Ross Parkes taught at Mary's during the summer—usually he taught at the National Institute of the Arts in Taipei, a school producing a whole crop of amazing dancers like Kun-Yang and Ruping Wang. Ross's classes were really tough. I loved to sweat.

Some of the modern classes I took after Graham included Colin Conner, Nicholas Leichter, Joy Kellman, Michael Foley, and Megan Williams. Sometimes I went over to Movement Research to check out Release Technique, but I could never figure out how to get my muscles moving in what I considered a floppy way. I loved workshops with Sara Pearson and while at Bates got to perform in the PearsonWidrig DanceTheater *Ordinary Festivals*—a dance-theater piece for three-hundred oranges, not as many dancers, and a couple of knives, all set in an Italian square to a score of pre-war Italian folk music.

I auditioned for David Dorfman, Carolyn Dorfman (no relation to David), Bebe Miller, Geulah Abrams (I got that one and worried about the rehearsal schedule all summer until I returned to NYC and discovered Geulah had suddenly died), John Freeman (got that one and we rehearsed in Spanish Harlem), José Limón, Paul Taylor, and Yael Lewin. (Got that last one by a word-of-mouth reference, not an audition, and then got fired when she watched me on videotape. I suggested during our phone interview that she might want to see me dance live, but she said that wasn't necessary. She watched me on video and fired me before we entered the studio. Then she saw me in performance and asked me to work with her, but I said, no, that was okay. It didn't seem necessary.) There were many names easily forgotten. One audition had a telephone interview prior to a studio call because the guy wanted to be sure I was okay dancing nude. I said, "That really depends on the art." He said, "But do you have a problem with nudity?" I said, "Not on principle." There were often dance auditions listed in *The Village Voice* for school education projects that interfered with regular jobs and weren't worth anything when listed on the résumé.

All along I worked with friends and colleagues such as Heather Harrington, Andrea Harris, Daniela, Sandra Kaufmann, and later the Antipodal Dancers. We danced in venues around town in informal showcases and formal performances and considered every forum an opportunity to be seen: Dance Theater Workshop, Dia Center for the Arts, which later became Joyce SoHo, St. Mark's, the Cunningham Studios, and P.S. 122, including the Graham studios, and other places. Once I even performed on cement in the basement of the Baby Doll Bar in the East Village. I was supposed to be a sea otter dancing to sea otter poetry. The poet spat at me as he provided a soundtrack with words about bubbles and water and furry creatures. I made twenty-five dollars.

The Bill T. Jones/Arnie Zane Dance Company audition stood out because everyone showed up for Bill's open cattle call at the City Center studios. With such a huge turnout, all I hoped was to make it to a callback. All types were there: Broadway dancers with their heavy makeup and nylons; ballet dancers pretending to be relaxed by wearing their hair in low ponytails; and the expected assortment of modern dancers of all shapes and sizes, different training backgrounds, and skill levels. Some modern dancers never shaved their armpits, and they were often from Germany or Sweden or France and living in New York City for a year. Lots of shapes and sizes were there because Bill T. has hired fat dancers. In reality, there is often only one spot for a large dancer in Bill's work, the role of the joker or jester, but she or he has to be well-trained. Sometimes that one dancer looks like the freak in Bill T.'s work.

At the audition I attended, there were only three staff members of the Bill T. Jones/Arnie Zane Dance Company behind a small card table. The organizers of Bill T.'s audition were frantically trying to deal with registering people, writing names down on a list and giving out white pieces of paper with numbers written quickly in black permanent marker on the front.

My number 99 bulged because of my breasts. I moved the paper to my hip. There was a long line of dancers snaking down the City Center stairway, and the fourth floor studio was packed with dancers stretching and warming up.

A woman wearing all black and knee-high leather Dr. Martens boots yelled from the doorway of the studio, "We're going to start: first one hundred numbers in the studio, please. The rest of you out here." For all her toughness, "please" sounded like a high-pitched squeak. She didn't seem to recognize any of the auditioning dancers. "What a piss-poor idea," I heard her say under her breath.

Bill T. was at the front of the studio, sitting in a folding chair. He looked pleased. All these people who audition are future audience members. Maybe he had no idea he was such a popular company among the masses. Maybe it's only because of the recent *New Yorker* article about his piece *Still/Here*. The masses don't always turn out for auditions, but Bill T. is an international touring company. He's been written up in all the major newspapers and is controversial because he is open about being HIV+. Everyone thinks coming to this audition on a Sunday morning, instead of going to church, which very few dancers attend anyway, is worth a shot. Then all these dancers go to future performances and make themselves feel better by criticizing anyone who gets into the company.

"Line up in order of your numbers," yelled the woman in combat boots.

We organized ourselves quickly. Once orders are given, dancers follow them very well. We are less adept at milling about without direction. It's a top down hierarchy in the dance world.

"Walk center stage, make a movement, say your name, walk off," instructed Bill T. "Present yourself. I want to see you."

Bill is a tall black man with an original way of moving, which is evident even when he walks. There is something that holds your eye. Even in the studio. He's a star.

Number one walked to center stage. She stumbled over her foot, making an improvisatory twirling movement and said her name, "Cecilia, Bill T., and I love your work!" She hopped into the air when she said, "work!"

Bill T. said, "Run to the center and say your name. Just your name. No extra movement."

A woman behind me muttered. "If we have to say our name, why hassle with the goddamn numbers?" It was a rhetorical question, never to be voiced to the director in control.

The line continued and the names blurred, a lone dancer running to the center of the studio looking alternately haggard or awkward, a coyote separated from the pack. Our spoken names sounded either as if we didn't know how to speak, or as if we were howling at our fate.

I ran to the center, my arms open in an expansive and generous second, and stopped dead center. Legs parallel, stomach pulled in. I looked straight at Bill T. He looked down at his sheet of paper and crossed numbers off his list with a red pen.

"Renée," I yelled.

I had nothing to lose—not even my dignity. Bill did not look up. I ran off to join the other 99 dancers at the side of the room.

All but two of us were cut, and another hundred dancers filed into the room.

I tried not to feel humiliated and to remind myself that Bill T. is really hard to get into. It's an artist's maxim, but I reminded myself, "You never know. You never know who will sign your next paycheck."

"Waste of time, girls," a woman wearing character shoes and long hoop earrings screamed at the waiting dancers outside the studio.

She inadvertently pushed me up against the card table where the staff members continued to register dancers. A woman wrote the number 403 on a square of white paper and handed it to a waiting dancer.

Act Eight

"Like a meteor shower [the Kevin Wynn Collection] was spectacular, beautiful, and potentially dangerous."

—Susan Kraft,
Staten Island Advance

Theatrical Release

There is no reason why a star burns out other than its time is up. When you see a star burn out in real time before your eyes, the sight and the sensation of sight travel toward you and stay with you, forever. Her name was Liz, but we called her Bruce. Bruce for Bruce Lee.

Liz was collected, firm, hard to taste.
She danced tough. Onstage, she held her own.

"It would be just like Liz to end dramatically," says a fellow dancer. "So theatrical. Everything a performance."

"She talked about doing it," says another.

Another phones me, sobbing: *Gone, gone, gone, gone. Néeeee.* My nickname is a wail.

"Breathe," I say. "Take a breath right now."

After I put down the phone, I go to the bathroom and throw up.

Despite being selfish and self-centered, narcissistic even, dancers are too giving, too generous to dance only to the tune of their own breath. So even if she danced alone—at home in the kitchen or the living room or the bedroom or in a single loft in Chinatown in New York City—she danced for you. The final performance of her life was not a theatrical event: it was a theatrical release from the pain of being trapped inside a body that could not move enough. If only her cells had been able to explode, and she had been able to keep herself alive. For it is the "I" in the end that keeps the self alive.

Sometimes so many stars burn out in a sky, it is impossible to comprehend each one. The sky opens and the light—it is white—descends to surround my entire body.

She could go over the front of her foot, land on her knee
without a sound, her back leg stretched behind her.

I could never do it. My Achilles didn't stretch far enough, and I was too scared. Too fearful of hurting myself. Liz wasn't. She didn't mind getting hurt, but once, I had my hair in a ponytail and whipped my head around, foot behind, demi-pointe, turning quickly. My ponytail smacked her in the face.

"Graham Cracker," Liz said, "would you mind putting up your hair." An order. Not a question. I saw a little welt on her cheek.

"I'm so sorry," I said. "I'm sorry. I didn't mean to."

In the end, when a life is gone, pleadings such as these mean nothing. I didn't realize how fearless she was; I didn't know that all the physical ones die. The sky opens. The fourth wall breaks. She is gone.

The light is immense, immaculate, full and empty all at the same time. I look down. I see so much and understand nothing. The light is there, surrounding me, and I am at peace.

"I hope she is finally at peace," an acquaintance, a dancer with poor feet, says. The comment is banal, arrogant, and pretentious. Clichés convey the incompetence of those who are out of touch with their own feelings. They do not know how to address the dead. They think there should be different phrases for the different ways people die. Who cares, though, how someone dies? Why ask? Once a person is dead, she is dead. Years later, my cousin writes the same phrase to me in an e-mail, in different circumstances, using a different pronoun for a different gender: "I hope he is finally at peace." The light descends then, too. I remember Liz, our Bruce, and her death. Regret does not let the dead live.

The walls were white at the cast party Bruce held for us. She stayed up late after performance the night before to make cookies. Dancers love cookies. Like puppies, they like treats. Liz paid for all the food and all the alcohol herself. She did not have poor feet. She could go over the arch of her foot and down to her knee. It is important not to glorify death, but why not?

The walls of her loft were white. Those who do not live in New York City but imagine they want to live there think the loft is romantic. Those who live in New York City know better. There was a hammock and rope in the corner. No one could see the rope or know its use. Now they feel they should have seen and should have known. Therapy teaches me that regret and guilt are different.

I remember the stairs up to the loft apartment. I remember the stove. The kitchen was open. I remember the small space for the bed and cloth curtains separating the open living area from the space for sleeping. I remember her first ballet teacher. He still teaches on the Upper East Side of Manhattan.

✖

Kevin Wynn sat at the front of the studio, looking over his notes, waiting for Liz and me to warm up. We'd stretched and done *pliés, grands pliés, tendus,* and *rond de jambes.* I'd even done *rond de jambes en l'air.* Circling the leg in a semi-circle warms up the hip before *grands battements;* after those, I lay down on the floor and circled my leg more aggressively, trying to warm up the hip area, especially the right side where sciatica often hits. If I got my hips warm enough, the glutes loose enough, Kevin's movement didn't spark the sciatica.

That night, Liz and I didn't talk as we warmed up. It was our first rehearsal alone with each other. With Kevin. Each dancer has her own way of getting the body going at nine o'clock at night, especially when morning class is at ten. It makes for a long day to start and stop dancing; the contraction and release of the muscles causes all the major ones to freeze like a package of peas that has taken the wrong shape. I noticed it particularly in my quads, which were getting too bulky. I was in the habit of clenching the muscles of my quads to lift my leg into extension, to get it really high, instead of turning out the leg using a spiral-like sensation which rotates the leg clockwise and allows it to lift, ostensibly effortlessly, at the same time. Dance teachers always yell "from the hip," but it just shows their inability to articulate muscular action in a manner that is useful to the dance student.

Liz looked down at me lying on the floor and did a little Irish step dance imitation of the leading man, Michael Flatley, in *Riverdance*. We called him "Rooster." Later he became *Lord of the Dance*. *Riverdance* was all the rage on Broadway, and we hated it. Liz mimicked the Irish dancing, her feet flying out in front, her hands straight down at her sides, and then tossed her head. I giggled. At the previous rehearsal, she told a story about how a distant relative asked her if she was going to appear in *Riverdance*. We all flopped to the floor laughing and kicking our legs in the air like ladybugs caught upside down.

Broadway was so different from modern, but anyone who didn't know the distinction always asked the same question, which each of us had heard from one of our mother's friends, "Do you dance on Broadway, dear?" What was the answer? "No, we dance in lofts and black boxes, and we don't wear nylons or character shoes when we take class." Of course, those Irish dancers were very good, and we told ourselves we didn't make fun of them because of their success, but only because we were all perpetually broke.

∞

After I saved enough money to fly home to see my parents in Idaho, I ran into the Sheriff's Deputy at Hay's Chevron. When he found out I was dancing in New York, he asked, "With a pole?"

"You can wish upon a star," I said.

It was a common question from older men. If someone didn't ask if I were on Broadway, he asked if I danced in a club. A club meant a strip club, which meant I would wear a thong, or a love-string, as I liked to call them, and not much else. My friends teased me that I had the boobs to do it. But no, I didn't dance with poles or take off my clothes. I knew dancers who did, though, even dancers without breasts. I knew of the rumor that School of American Ballet students danced in Times Square, before Times Square was Disney, and that lots of Joffrey dancers, when Joffrey was based in New York instead of Chicago, made money in the seedy places—five-hundred to one-thousand bucks a night. I remembered one of my first ballet teachers, who danced for Harkness Ballet, now defunct, making references to the money she'd made late at night. I never made any money from dancing. Not with a pole, not with my clothes on or off, and not on Broadway. I was off-Broadway, or as Liz and I joked with each other, we were off-off-off-off-off Broadway.

One of my mother's high school friends, who chose the unfortunate time of visiting during my vacation to Idaho, said, "All dancers have anorexia. You'll want to watch your weight."

"My mind, you mean," I said.

"No, really, don't starve yourself to death," she said, eating another one of my mother's chocolate chip cookies. "Anorexia is a slow form of suicide." The chocolate melted on her lip and a black spot stayed there the rest of the evening.

Suicide is not always a cry for help, I wanted to say. Sometimes it's an understandable release. Besides, all dancers are not anorexic. I wanted to explain that both clichés are an easy way to dismiss a dancer's voice. Dancers aren't supposed to speak up, so they don't. I couldn't even find my voice to counter the dismissive generalizations made by my mother's friend.

Liz was Korean-American. Her eyes were curtain scrims. There was mystery behind each scrim, and danger, too, and passion. Her eyes would have been called smoky in another context, or exotic in another era. When Bruce

Lee stretches his body back and extends his front leg, the leg twists inward as if it could drill into its object, his eyes narrow and open all at once. There is nowhere else to look.

She danced like a boxer: fast in, quick out,
always going back for more. Her feet intricate.

That night, I bent my left leg, grabbed my right ankle and crossed it over my left knee, then raised that knee until I felt the pull across my right glute muscles. Then I let the knee fall a little to the left, a little more pull, especially at the point of twist in my spine, around L4, right near scar tissue from an old injury. When I stretched to the right, there was no pull at all in my glutes. I switched sides and repeated the action. Then I rolled each ankle in circles in succession, eight clockwise, eight counter-clockwise, repeat. Flex and point, flex and point ten times. Then flex the leg up to the ceiling, heel first, and down to the floor, heel to butt. Again, up and down, four more times. Keeping the leg straight up, just one leg in the air, I pressed my chin to my chest, arms off the floor at my sides, and pressed down over and over with my arms, palms down. It was a perverted way to do the Pilates strengthening exercise, but it felt useful and warmed up my stomach muscles without having to move my back.

I don't like Pilates—I mean the way Joseph Pilates looks—so I feel no compunction changing his exercises to suit myself or combining them with a Floor Barre approach. I don't know why middle-aged, middle-class women want to do exercises that create fireplug bodies and strengthen flexion over extension. Perhaps they've never seen a picture of Joseph Pilates standing in his red box-like underwear, his muscles bulging, looking like an overgrown and underdressed gnome.

"You Graham people love the floor, don't you," Liz said, laughing.

"Can't seem to get off it." I laughed.

As soon as he heard us talking, Kevin said, "Ready, ladies?"

Liz turned, immediately at attention. Warm-up was over. I rolled over to standing and took my place next to Liz. We didn't leave the same amount of distance the Graham dancers always left between themselves and the rehearsal director or the teacher. We stood close to Kevin because we always wanted to hug him. I often found myself starting to hold onto his sweater sleeve the way I used to hold onto my mother's sleeve or pant leg when I was kid.

Liz arched her upper body back, extended her front leg toward Kevin, the leg twisted inward as if the leg itself could drill into its object.

"Okay, Bruce," said Kevin, "start with A."

Kevin made a clicking sound with his tongue in three-quarter time, a waltz essentially, though in this context it should be called a post-modern waltz. He tapped the toes of his heavy leather Caterpillar boots on the floor. Kevin never rehearsed with music. Philip Hamilton would compose live music for this piece, and we'd combine the live music with the dance at dress rehearsal the night before opening.

Liz, her eyes narrow and open at the same time, started an eight-count phrase. Halfway through, at the dancer's count of 4 2/3, Kevin said, "Okay, Née, start B." Kevin kicked his left leg out, slightly, to indicate the start of the phrase.

I kicked my left leg out, circled it in a *rond de jambe,* which I made up because I couldn't remember the correct movement, then hit my stride as my body started moving from memory. Characteristic Kevin arms flew across each other, one arm around my head while the other circled my waist. When I was about to turn, not a circle in the intuitively clockwise direction, but counter-clockwise against the flow of a right-handed person, Kevin said, "Stop. There."

Liz instinctively reached her hand out, and I grabbed it, taking Liz's full weight while she extended her leg to second and sat to the floor at the same time. I'm not sure how we knew what to do, except that we knew this was how Kevin worked. He taught us his phrases, his arms, his legs, and then he needed to see them moving in combination so he could adjust, usually not the movement itself, but the phrasing or spacing or direction or partnering. We moved for him to give him what he needed.

Other choreographers could spend hours on three steps. With Kevin, we never spent time endlessly discussing a particular movement, those anal discussions about whether a flexed foot means anger or a *coupé* a submission to love. That was a waste of everyone's time and a waste of their bodies. Kevin didn't agonize over the meaning of three steps. He wanted movement. Dancing.

I held Liz's weight; no way would I let Liz fall on my watch. Thank goodness the soles of my feet were dirty and stuck to the wooden floor. The rehearsal space at Evolving Arts had a particularly slippery floor. They waxed and buffed it to a shine that was nightmarish to dance on. Daniela had told me the new crop of Isadorables rehearsed there, too, but they liked the sheen because it helped them produce a sliding effect for Isadora Duncan's flowing Grecian movements. But for Kevin's urban, sometimes combative movement the shiny wooden floor was terrible. We needed to be able to hold our ground and hold someone else's weight.

"Okay, let's go back," said Kevin.

Née: The rock.
Bruce: The river.

We started our phrases from the beginning, putting in a little more emphasis at certain parts, claiming the steps into our bodies. The "A" phrase person was the mover, the river; the "B," the rock. I watched Liz circle her phrase around me.

A back side front, turn, fall to the floor,
roll over her back to standing.

At the point where she stood with her back to mine, Kevin said, "There. Stop. Hold it a moment."

Kevin was a big man, warm and generous, his movement intricate and full. The rehearsal process for Kevin's pick-up company was long and fun. It was the only time I really felt a choreographer wanted to see my body play. I always wished I could have seen him dance with the Limón Company. He'd left Limón because performance terrified him; sometimes he didn't even watch performances of his own company but sat in a nearby bar and came back for final bows.

At the first performance of his work that I had ever seen, the audience was made up of dancers. Dancers were often the only people who attended performances, but these were all different kinds of dancers—the whole dance community. Everyone loved Kevin. Okay, not everyone. Some critics thought his work didn't have a story. Does modern urban life have a story? It is a coming together and a separating, a partnering duet or a trio, a betrayal, an individual solo, a walking down the street alone with others walking next to you, a return, concrete beneath your feet, your dance bag heavy across your shoulders, everyone striving for something and finding their art and not finding anything at all. You don't know the story of each person whom you meet, but you do know how she moves. You can see it. *Keep it cool, kid. Keep it cool.*

Some said his work was a big massive dance party; consequently, it was too hard to follow and too fast to see anything. He didn't allow moments. What were his human sculptures then? Does living in New York City allow moments, I asked one critic, or is it one massive swirl of humanity? No and yes, she said. Well, then, I said, now you understand his choreography.

Other critics had different impressions: "A high voltage maelstrom of movement," appeared in *The Village Voice;* "An absolute knockout," in *The New York Times.* The review clip that described his movement best, from a dancer's point-of-view, was by Lisa Jo Sagolla in *Backstage:* "Wynn's difficult-to-do choreography calls on every aspect of a dancer's physical technique, yet demands only that which is kinesthetically natural."

When you are dancing for a choreographer who loves his dancers, you don't think about the critics. It was true, there was a lot happening onstage, which is why it was so much fun: tons of all-out, balls-to-the-wall dancing, trios and duets and quartets all at the same time. To Kevin, we were each unique. He knew our bodies. Or we felt he did, which is the same thing. If I couldn't dance with Jiří Kylián and Nederland's Dans Theater, I was lucky to dance with Kevin.

We all knew Bruce was his fearless muse. Liz got a solo that was not back grounded by a clump of moving bodies like most of the other solos in Kevin's work. Liz was alone, onstage, and we all crowded the wings to watch. *She danced tough. Hard to taste.* I loved to watch her so much in rehearsals with the entire pick-up group that sometimes I missed the steps Kevin gave to me. Stef filled me in later, after rehearsal. Stef absorbed Kevin's movement into her body like it was cotton candy. So did Alenka, a silky creature moving through time and space, spinning off before the solos; she had trained in Europe and at Ailey, so unlike me, she was flexible in body, mind, and spirit. What Kevin called his pick-up group worked as a testing ground: for many, like Marc, like Stef, who both went on to Bill T. Jones, it was the penultimate stage before major touring companies; for others, like me, like Liz, though she also danced for Eun Me Ahn and Bebe Miller, it was the ultimate stage before leaving dance.

In the rehearsal for our duet, with no one else present, Kevin told me to stand up on Liz's back and roll off head first, no arms. I couldn't do it, so I stood stock still. Like a stork. Couldn't even shake my head: No. I could not fall from that height to the floor.

Kevin slapped his thigh. "Never seen that before," he said. But he didn't reprimand me.

Liz flopped over to the floor and waved her legs in the air, laughing. I could feel my face flush. Finally, I shook my head.

"*I'll* get on *her* back," said Liz.

Kevin said, gently, "Okay, Née, be the rock."

I got down on my hands and knees and knitted my stomach tight. Liz stepped up on my back. She was a good dancer—putting one foot on my sacrum and one foot on my upper back—not one of those bridge and tunnel dancers who would have put both feet on my lower back, causing injury. Sure-footed. Swift-footed Achilles. Except he was a guy. But his ghost did visit Odysseus. Does her ghost visit Kevin?

It was November, the performance run wasn't until January, but I knew what we worked on tonight could be in the show even though Kevin might not place it until a week or two before opening night. Then Liz would remember the entire combination, her part, A, and my part, B, and reconstruct it for me, quickly, so that we were ready. If I forgot the steps in performance, the steps not being in my body the way Kevin's movement was in Liz's pores—she'd even whisper to me in performance: step right, back, around, kick it out, grab the hand, head down, kick it over, stand, walk away, turn back, step back, fall. Down to the floor I'd fall and roll, and stand up quickly into parallel position with my arms at my sides. Mountain pose, but we didn't call it that.

Now, Liz would say, her back to the audience so they couldn't see her pucker her lips at me: step back, my turn!

I looked up from my position as rock and watched her explore for him. This was my first rehearsal with only Kevin and Liz. It would be our last. Somehow, we got through the duet. Instead of glaring at me afterward for the lapse in my body memory, Liz winked. Our secret.

Kevin decided not to partner Liz and me for the duet he'd created on us after all. Kevin put me with Stef, my friend, and Liz with Lara, her friend. Liz reconstructed the duet and taught it to Lara. Kevin set a new one on Stef and me that had a lot to do with our differences in height and ability to lift each other; although, all Kevin's dancers had to be able to lift and partner all different sizes and shapes. His choreography was egalitarian that way. Democratic and non-gendered. A male crotch or female crotch in your face, white or black or brown, it made no difference. But it made a difference to the audience. All those colors and shapes combined and reconstructed.

There's a synchronicity when friends dance together, a lightness where competition intermixes with love, and corrections are given by teasing or asking: *Hey, love,* Stef murmurs, *why not grab my hand here,* an arm indicates the movement, *instead of here,* a leg indicates a latter phrase. In our duet, I had to drop to my knees at the same moment Stef kicked over my head; if our timing was off, Stef would kick me in the head or, worse, the neck. I waited as long as possible to duck, daring Stef to kick too soon, and Stef smiled, her legs so long, so powerful, she controlled me with her limbs. After I ducked, I reached both arms overhead. Stef pulled hard, while I jumped, from a crouch up into her arms.

Both Stef and Liz had pale brown-colored skin, different tones, and black hair; although Stef's was crinkly and wild, Liz's cropped and straight. Later, after Bill T., when Stef was dancing in Europe, Pina Bausch picked her up for a project. Stef is that gorgeous. Privately, Stef and I called ourselves a fusion of coffee and milk. Stef was espresso with an occasional lemon twist. Because of my weight, I was half-and-half. I'd lost my scholarship at the Graham School because I'd gained five pounds.

Never should have gone to Graham. Should have gone to Limón. Should have gone to Europe. Should have tried to get into the Mark Morris Dance Group. Should have studied longer with men instead of bitter women. I'd understudied *Panorama,* but then hadn't been cast when the Graham Company took the piece, with thirty women from the school, to the Spoleto Festival. Thirty bitchy young female dancers in *Panorama,* and I was cut because I was too fat. Before rehearsals started I'd renewed my passport, so I was ready to travel; I was positive they would use me after all the time I spent understudying at City Center. But the five pounds kept me home, in the city, while one of my friends had an affair in Italy with a sound guy (a true affair, she was married).

I lost five pounds; Graham didn't reinstate my scholarship, so I lost five more, vowed to finish their program, and move on. Martha Graham was dead and operatic. Kevin Wynn was alive and current.

After her return from Argentina, I'd started working with Daniela. She was no longer interested in choreographing a post-modern *Firebird*, but was engaged in entirely new work. "Straight from my subconscious to your body," she said.

At another rehearsal, Daniela had said, her Argentinean accent slurring the words slightly, "Doll, you must go to the Kevin Wynn Collection. Borges in the dance. Will flip you." Daniela was given over to odd constructions, sometimes, like the time she became the Firebird. But then she became human again. Stood upright. Continued choreographing.

Daniela had been asked to join the Isadorables after she returned from Argentina, and she'd started to wear a tunic to our rehearsals, too, for her own choreography, which we were performing at various showcases. Given what had happened to Daniela before, her parents didn't want her to leave home again, but once Daniela was out of the wheelchair she got right back into the dance studio. She got back on the horse that threw her, so to speak.

Daniela told me she didn't plan on using Stravinsky ever again. "Get reservations to Kevin Wynn," she said.

The performance flipped me, I went back to Dance Theater Workshop two nights in a row, and suddenly I had direction, a company I wanted to join, a reason to lose yet another five pounds.

By the time I got in Kevin's pick-up company, after shadowing his classes for several years, most of the dancers I'd seen in that first concert, including Kun-Yang Lin, had already moved on to other choreographers. But Marc Mann was in that first performance I saw and still with Kevin when I joined.

"Pedestrian, girl," Marc advised after my first rehearsal with Kevin, "keep it simple. Walk it."

"It's hard," Kun-Yang said when I ran into him at ballet class in the morning at 580 Broadway, "after the aggressive push and struggle and strain of Graham."

Graham had given me an abdomen. I could stand on two feet without falling over. I couldn't stand on Liz's back and fall off, but I had found my center. For now. I sent all my previous dance teachers postcard announcements for Kevin Wynn's *Super Bon Bon* run at DTW. I made sure to include the college teacher whose contortionist choreography had injured my back and who told me I crashed to the floor and smiled too much.

> *She made it into* The New York Times,
> The Village Voice.

Both Lara and I had white skin, blonde hair, though Lara liked to color her short hair different shades of red. I never colored my long hair. Liz and Lara partnered downstage right. Stef and I partnered upstage left. Lara and Liz and Stef all knew how to "walk it"; they'd studied with Kevin at SUNY Purchase. On the SUNY Purchase College Conservatory of Dance website, Liz is listed as alumni—"with the angels." For the parallel duets, Liz and Lara were already onstage, downstage, in the spotlight.

After a mass combustion, a traffic jam or a subway squeeze, where Kevin piled ten dancers on top of each other, Liz emerged from the mêlée and kept spinning until Lara joined her. Stef and I waited until the stage cleared of the other dancers, and we ran on from opposite sides, second wing. We always took a beat when we joined each other before we started moving. Kevin preferred it that way, but Stef and I milked it for all its worth. Some of the dancers were really good at the beat—Stef was one, striking a pose and shooting a dagger at the audience—but others stumbled into the beginning of a phrase. I always pretended to be one of Barry Flanagan's huge bronze rabbit sculptures, which were currently on view along Park Avenue. Flanagan had a piece called *Large Mirror Nijinski,* two rabbits seemingly in motion with both arms raised and one leg extended, looking at each other across the street. I tried to explain to Stef that she could be one Nijinski and I could be the other rabbit, but she thought I was nuts.

"What, girl," Stef asked, "you want me to pretend to be a faun?"

"A rabbit," I said.

Stef hadn't walked along Park Avenue for a long time.

Flanagan also had two permanent rabbits on 53rd Street, which I had walked by every morning on my way to Graham, and often visited now, so sometimes I took the shape of the one I called the *Tai Chi Rabbit,* thinking it was a nice counterpart to Liz's *Bruce Lee* on the other side of the stage. I lifted my right knee, right ankle on the bent knee of the supporting leg, extended my arms, and focused my eyes as if I were doing Tai Chi. No one really knew what the hell I was talking about when I waxed poetic about bronze rabbit sculptures and dance.

Kevin still liked to tease me, "Née," he might say, "are you *Thinker on a Rock* today?"

I could never get away from pretending to be some kind of animal; it was a hangover from Graham.

The two duets downstage and upstage were supposed to start moving together, but once we were in performance, Bruce and Lara always started before Stef and I were in place. It pissed Stef off because they hadn't done it that way in rehearsal. Stef thought Bruce and Lara were claiming glory, but I thought it was funny. Does an audience look at the dancer who is moving or at the one who is standing still? I took my rabbit pose and gazed adoringly at Stef. Movement was free with her. I'd spent too many years withering at Graham. *Let it go,* Stef sometimes whispered to me; I'd breathe and relax and let it go. *Oh yeah,* she'd say.

After our parallel duets, Liz stayed onstage for her solo. She was exhausted by then, but Philip Hamilton drummed her onward. Liz threw her right leg around to a lunge—an open, extended Fourth position—and took a moment to look out at the audience. She did not see their faces, she was already gone, into the dance, but they saw hers. Bruce had that power. The power to stay with you long after the performance is over. Then she rolled over the top of her front foot, her knee hitting the floor with no sound whatsoever, threw her back right leg around her body, spinning in a circle as if she were a top, and exploded back to standing, limbs flying everywhere, stopping still in the same Fourth position. The audience gasped—how could she move that way? Liz was a being out of *Crouching Tiger, Hidden Dragon*. She lives.

> *The effort in her body—not her face.*
> *Not until the end.*

We went on tour, and Liz warned me, "Watch out for the sound guy, I've partied with him." Still, Stef and I partied with him at a topless bar that made me feel I had a flat chest. We ended up running through sprinklers with our clothes on at 3 a.m. It seemed like the thing to do while on tour in Florida. I didn't know that the Florida tour really was to be my last performance with Kevin—on a huge proscenium stage and real lights and a Marley floor. Lara smacked me so hard during the performance I got a shiner on my forehead and had to perform my solo in a daze. The costume was a tiny pair of brown Lycra shorts and a cropped tank top. My butt was firm, and I wore my Wonder Woman bra that held my non-dancer breasts tightly in place. *Fame*, we teased each other before the curtain rose, *I wanna live forever.*

> *In the end, Liz's boyfriend, also a dancer,*
> *found her in her loft apartment.*

Liz's boyfriend helped her down to the floor. Her feet were bare; she wore no socks. Once he enfolded her body into his, the way they had practiced many times, there was nothing left to do but cry. So he did. She had leaned back, heavy with weight, and he pulled her close, raising her bare feet off the dance floor, encircling her with his arms, folding her head next to his neck, her breath warm and sweet on his skin. Except now there was no warm breath. As he folded her into him, there was no sweet breath at all.

She wanted him to quiet the sway of her body,
the swings of her mood, the thinness of her being.

He is strong. A powerful mover. Lifter. Muscles. He might have said, "What have you done, my love?" speaking to her out loud. He might have pulled her body into his arms, cradling her. His body shook. Tears fell down his face onto her face. The fluid from his body had too much life for him now, but not enough for both of them. No, no, no, no, no, he repeated to himself. His body shook. Her body was still. No. Change action. Change time. Go back. Do phrase A. No. Stop there.

Some thought the concert should have been canceled. But the show must go on. The show always goes on.

He let her down to the floor, felt her wrists,
her lack of breath. Kissed her pale brown face.

I become the earth and watch her moving across the sky. An arm here. A leg there. Phrase A. Phrase B. Makes no difference. A full constellation suspended in the arms and legs of the *tour jeté*. It is a swirling Capoeira movement, head down.

The burning of the star affects others in the sky. Down below, the force of this explosion makes us reverberate and circle. As if we are onstage alone with a spot, we try to find the center of the light. For those who are left behind, it becomes a dull search. Others might want to burn out by their own hand but cannot because she has already gone in a blaze before, and they have seen the pain.

At first, the pain is felt as if a meteor shoots through the top of your skull and rips out what you held most dear. You begin looking for what is dear in all the wrong places. You walk in a daze. Some keep dancing. Others do not.

Only someone who has gone before knows to raise the scrim, look you straight in the eyes, and say, "I do not know what to say."

Her whole life an effort to carve space
by shaping the negative air around her.

Not on Broadway. Not with a pole. Not in a black box. In a field far from New York City, I am dancing.

I am dancing under the stars. After a *rond de jambe en l'air,* I take a wide and open Fourth position. Look up.

There is the dancer Liz whose nickname was Bruce Lee and who lived a short time, yet long enough to burn out so brightly the light lingers and does not fade and travels still.

Act Nine

"[Shawn] used to say that every American should have to stand naked in Times Square one day a year—then America would be a nation of beautiful bodies."

—Mary Kerner,
Barefoot to Balanchine

Holy Feet

Ted carried a four-by-four foot Marley dance floor around New York City. The floor was made of heavy duty, slip-resistant linoleum. Rolled up, it looked like a yoga mat in a purple pouch, but the dance floor was much thicker and much heavier than a yoga mat. When the spirit moved him, or when someone pissed him off, he'd throw down his floor right in the middle of the sidewalk. People had to walk around him, or stop and watch.

Usually Marley floors were gray or black, especially the ones dance companies used for travel. Ted's floor was light brown. He took to wearing matching brown tights and a bicep-revealing T-shirt. He never put out a black felt Busker hat, or any hat at all, because he believed in donating his services for the general benefit of art.

What he did could be called education or craziness, depending on the movement or the place in the city. If he threw down his floor in Times Square, in the summer, his routine came across as free expression, part of the teeming mass of the city; if in Coney Island, in the fall, he came across as a man who missed his time in the circus.

Ted threw down his floor, and he moved his hips first. Forward, if someone made him angry. Side to side, if someone made him happy. The tights revealed all. Then he started moving his head in free form, a combination of wham-bam-thank-you-ma'am jazz and Isadora Duncan ecstasy, fantastical sideways and circular motions, around and around until it looked like the head—his head—started to fall off.

Isadora Duncan lost her head because she loved wearing long scarves. The red scarf with painted yellow autumn leaves and eighteen inch fringes on either end caught on the spokes of the red convertible, an Amilcar, not a Bugatti, as others have written, her scarf trailing in the wind only momentarily, the brief moment of a life. Isadora's head was pulled back, fantastically wrenched into extension, and the world lost the other thread of modern dance. Ted loved that image. He often used it on the street.

After Isadora died, the focus concentrated on that other woman, Martha, and her ugly, staccato, contractions. Ugly is supposed to generate response—an emotional response in the viewer that makes one feel a wrenching in the gut similar to the wrenching felt in the dancer's gut. Without Isadora to breathe for the wind, dance lost its flow and musicality and ecstatic origins.

Ted had studied the Martha Graham technique. Briefly. He was too much the jester, the wisest one around, to succeed at Graham, but he could have played King Lear's fool. Of course, Martha re-interpreted the Greeks—not Shakespeare—and always from the point of view of the woman, the ugly woman. There was no role for Ted in her ballets, and he knew it.

Like the historical Ted Shawn, with whom he shared a first name, Ted believed in the ministry of dance. The difference, though, was that Ted Shawn had started divinity studies and never worn a collar, but the contemporary Ted had completed his studies and worn the white constraint.

When he first moved to the city from the Midwest, leaving his Lutheran collar behind, Ted had taken the Corvino ballet classes, religiously, starting his training with the father, who later became a ballet master for Pina Bausch Tanztheater, and continuing with the daughters. Ted still took a Corvino class every Saturday at 580 Broadway when a live pianist played for class. A live pianist is standard fare in NYC dance classes; without one, dancers do not show up. With his living room turned dance studio, Ted easily could have done all his training and rehearsals at home. But he didn't have a piano.

Ted aimed to bring back the ecstatic in modern dance. This was his new ministry. There was an aspect of God in everything he did, even if what he did wasn't successful. Ted threw his floor down on the sidewalk across from the Orpheum Theatre on Second Avenue, even though he doesn't particularly like the show *Stomp*. He begins.

It doesn't really matter if there is an audience or not because in his former life he was a Lutheran minister. He always dreamed of being a modern dancer, though no one, including himself, is sure how he got the dream. Even his mother doesn't know. After he moved to the city, he didn't go to church again, but he did *pliés* every single day thereafter. Ted was taught to preach whether or not anyone showed up. God still hears your words, he was taught. This knowledge carries over into his new profession. Dance whether or not anyone shows up. God still sees your body move. Ted dances on a street corner and wiggles his hips and walks the square of his dance floor and stares out at the traffic on Second Avenue. Taxi horns and pedestrian footsteps become the musical score for Ted's dances.

Ted can't do any of the clown repertoire, so he pretends. He can't really walk a tightrope or a loose rope or down into a trunk or up into the moon. He can't really make us feel his loneliness, although he tries, and often we do. But when people stop to watch Ted on the street corner, puzzlement masks their faces. They do not know what to think. Nevertheless, Ted is a performer. He notices the faces watching him. From Martha, he has learned how to stand still and command attention, so he does that for a while.

I imagine I saw him once, with his floor, on the sidewalk. I watch, without announcing my presence. It was long past the time that I had danced with Ted and Claire, long past the time that I'd injured my shoulder lifting Claire, long past the time I felt guilty when I didn't take daily class or do *pliés* in my studio apartment.

Ted takes a step forward, to the edge of the Marley dance floor, raises his arms overhead and juts his right hip out of joint. The graceful position of his arms is a distinct contrast to the distorted position of his hips. His aggressive expression, almost a frown, says, "This is my body. What are you going to do about it?"

Gradually an audience forms around him. Ted continues to step and thrust his hip left or right, moving his arms gracefully to Fifth position with each step. It could be an imitation of an ugly duckling learning to walk, out of his natural environment on a New York City street.

I thought there was a charisma about Ted, a poignant charm, and I was always transfixed by his focus. He was a force out of the sixties, out of place in nineties New York, a man out of step with his dreams.

Ted had legs that were well balanced and in proportion to the rest of his body. He had wide feet, with a good arch, because he had worked at it. His hands were as wide as his feet, and as expressive, and had he started dancing earlier there is no question he would have made it into a major company. Ted had forceful, strong movement, and he wasn't afraid to fail or to fall, occasionally throwing his body to the floor (or the street) with such force we would gasp until he broke his fall with his hands, lightly landing on them as if they were feet. He wore his brown hair alternately long, and free, or cut short, and proper. By the time I danced with him, he had a small balding spot on the back of his head.

Other dancers speak of him with awe. They are very impressed that he has taken dancing to the streets. Not through the program "Dancing in the Streets" with grants from the Lila Wallace Reader's Digest Fund, on various stages around New York City, but actually to the street itself, to different neighborhoods. Ted has freed his body. His mind no longer controls what is and isn't art. The other dancers in the company he and Claire formed, the Antipodal Dancers, are impressed. Modern dance is an elite art form, they know, and they applaud Ted's perseverance. They applaud him putting his body in other people's way, as if modern dance could be guerrilla theatre, as if modern dance could change the world, make it stop, make it take notice of the way we move through our lives.

It takes dancers to applaud the art of the street, but the pedestrians watching simply do not get what Ted is about. He isn't like that mime who pretends to be the Statue of Liberty, painted all green, and found at the South Street Seaport or in Times Square, depending on the day or the season. He isn't like the Latin dancer in the 42nd Street Station who dances with a lady puppet. He isn't like the Naked Cowboy in his tighty-whities and cowboy boots and cowboy hat. The reverent dancer Ted isn't like the Ghetto Original Dance Company who moved their break dancing and hip hop from Columbus Circle into P.S. 122 and then on to the New Victory Theater.

Ted is just a former minister without a shtick and with a love of moving and putting his body in people's faces. Maybe he should try wearing his collar when he dances.

Ted answers the question of whether dance is a young people's game or not. If we're trained in one approach and one aesthetic, we automatically blind ourselves to any other possibility. Liz Lerman Dance Exchange goes on and on, and her projects involve community, people who love to shake, rattle, and roll, people who want to express themselves, people whose thighs and tummies wiggle and shake when they dance. Who cares if one man's gesture is another man's death? We can tell when art is bad—when it doesn't fit our aesthetic—but can we tell when it is off-center?

Ted was off-center, some said past his prime, but who knew what his prime was anyway? He was preaching the gospel during his dancing prime. Maybe that was God's plan—to free him through his body. His pecs were strong; he could lift. I like anyone who can lift me.

Before Ted decided to take art to the people, he spent years performing with the Antipodal Dancers in the Antipodal Gallery in SoHo. We spent hours rehearsing in Ted's Park Slope apartment. He'd converted the living room into a dance studio with the same dimensions as the SoHo gallery in which we performed. The fourth wall was covered with a floor to ceiling mirror. The mirror was pretty good. It didn't distort much and even took a few pounds off the thighs.

Ted had gotten a deal on the mirrors when American Ballet Theatre updated their Broadway studios above where Ted took class with the Corvinos. Ted had hired glass movers to do the job, and he said it was like how he imagined moving art, a delicate process made superstitious by the knowledge that in this case the art was glass.

At the same time, Ted had purchased the Marley floor from ABTII, which he rolled up at the front of the living room when we weren't rehearsing. Most dancers have very little furniture. Their living rooms are bare stage sets. There must be room to move, but even if you are sitting, there must be room to contemplate. If there is too much furniture, it is too hard to think. The body begins to feel crowded. The cells over stimulated. The mini floor Ted rolled up in a bag and carried around Manhattan came from extras of his living room turned studio floor.

℘

The whole troupe of Antipodal Dancers spread out on the floor, warming up. Ted didn't mind coffee cups on his Marley dance floor—it was an old one, particularly sticky—and I had a cup from the Two Little Red Hens Bakery. Each birthday, Claire bought a cake from there, and we ended rehearsal early to celebrate or mourn the passage of another year. In a dancer's life, the center cannot hold. Ellen, Ted's partner, and I had already started on barre, but Claire, the group's co-founder with Ted, still lay on the floor. She'd had a lot more Graham training than the rest of us, so it was even harder for her to get off the floor. She'd also studied a lot more ballet than I had, so once she realized she could dance lying down, she never wanted to do anything else. Claire's long brown hair was loose all around her. She had worn it clipped back for so long she said she couldn't trap her hair any longer.

Ted had built the barre Ellen and I now used. He worked as a carpenter for his day job. Ted's barre had the most solid construction of any since the one I'd used as a kid. When I was a kid and started in ballet, my dad had built a barre in the dining room, so I could practice on the weekends.

"Shall we begin?" Ted asked.

Always dancers begin formally with a polite request. It takes the edge off of the hard work. It doesn't lessen the sweat.

Ellen and I lifted the barre and carried it to the corner of the room. Claire put on the music. Ted took a position, and we sat in a semi-circle around him. He was the lead choreographer for this project; we, the women, were the chorus. We'd still develop the movement collaboratively, using Authentic Movement, and Ted would shape it, making the final decisions.

Ted's eyes closed. He began to move. He flexed his foot up and down. He flexed his hand up and down. We'd all agreed Ted needed a three-minute solo as part of the piece. It was a piece based on an oil painting of a red door. The solo would represent Ted walking barefoot through the door. The painting was called *New Red Door*.

"Keep going," Ellen said, encouragingly.

"Don't interrupt me," said Ted.

Claire had recorded Massenet's "Meditation" from *Thais* on loop, so it played over and over and over. The violin adagio relaxed me; I felt my eyes closing. I sat, straight backed, forcing my eyes to stay open, forcing myself to witness art in the making. It's a slow, tedious process, the making of art, but one must bear witness to the movement of the soul. Otherwise, what's the point? Especially if, in the end, the audience doesn't get it. And often, the audience doesn't get it.

The next rehearsal, Ted asked us to sit in a circle before we started improvising.

"Listen," Ted said, "How would you feel if the costume for my solo was nudity?"

Ellen said, "Really, Ted, your mother is coming from Minnesota to see you dance for the first time. Like I said before, I don't think you want her to see you naked."

"As a baby," Ted answered.

"She probably has a good idea what you look like now," Ellen said.

"It's my coming out," said Ted.

"You're not gay," said Ellen. "It's not your coming out."

Occasionally at rehearsal, Ted and Ellen had to work out some aspect of their relationship. If Claire and I realized soon enough that the volley was about to start, we just kept quiet. Dancers are very good at not saying anything. Talk back, speak up, you get fired. Simple. You can only talk back if you're involved with some aspect of production.

"My mom is coming to see me dance for the first time. I want to be completely exposed when I dance for her," Ted said.

"Then dance for her, but keep your clothes on. Nudity isn't part of this piece."

"As I walk through the red door in the painting, I become my real self. Me. Naked."

"Naked isn't a costume," Ellen retorted.

"It's the original costume. God's finest work." Ted pointed to the ceiling. To God.

Ellen uncrossed and opened her legs. She leaned forward. "Look, this isn't the bully pulpit. It's a dance piece for a tiny art gallery in SoHo."

"All the more reason to show myself as I really am. My aesthetic demands loyalty to the principle of the piece. The principle is self revealed."

"You're talking like a dancer now. I have no idea what you mean." Ellen straightened her back, opened her legs on the floor to a wide second. Even for a dancer, she was incredibly flexible. She had trouble with her knees hyper-extending because of her flexibility.

"A naked body is a beautiful body. A naked body reveals the self," said Ted.

"So, we'll put it in the program notes, and you can keep your clothes on," suggested Ellen. She could be very practical.

"My costume is nudity. God's work."

"Your costume is a Lycra unitard. I'll make it a pretty color. Your naked forty-eight-year-old body belongs in the bedroom where your wang can flop around at your whim. Your flopping wang does not belong in your mother's face."

"It does if it's part of the piece."

"And if it's not? What do you lose?" asked Ellen. "Nothing. What do you gain? Your dignity, for Chrissakes."

"Don't take the Lord's name in vain," said Ted.

"Don't be gratuitous in your mother's face," said Ellen.

"Look, you're just saying that I don't have a Pilobolus body, so I shouldn't go naked."

"You don't have a Pilobolus body," said Ellen. "I don't see you dancing for that company. Second of all, last I looked we call ourselves the Antipodal Dancers."

Claire reached over and pressed the pause button on Massenet.

"I'm talking about the integrity of the piece," said Ted, softly.

"I'm talking about your mother sitting and watching your wang flop around, which is exactly what will happen without your dance belt. She'll look away so she doesn't have to look at the flip-flopping, which will be completely out of time to the music, and everyone else will look away, too."

Claire and I avoided looking at each other. Dancers are very good at not looking at each other when rehearsal becomes stressful. They are very good at the art of control, at not showing what they are thinking. *Tabula rasa*—a beautiful blank body.

"David Parsons went nude," Ted said.

"Come on, if you had that body, you'd go nude, too."

"You're such a prude," said Ted.

"No, I'm not," said Ellen. "I have a point. Your member will flop around out of rhythm, and it will be distracting. Your dick won't keep time to the music unless you hold it. And that would be disgusting."

"I'll wear my dance belt. Naked otherwise."

"I'm listed as the Costume Designer on the program. You'll wear your goddamn unitard. It shows everything you've got anyway, for Chrissakes."

"Don't take the Lord's name in vain."

Ellen got up and walked into the kitchen. We could hear the tap running. She came back and stood at the side of the room with a glass of water.

Ted turned to Claire and said, "Music. Again. I must dance."

He began to dance, to explore with his eyes closed. Slowly he took off his T-shirt, took off his brown tights, it was hard to keep dancing as he did it, and then he stopped and opened his eyes.

"Oh God," he said. "Naked isn't part of the piece at all."

Ted stood in his dance belt, his legs together, his hands on his thighs, and he began contorting his face, opening and closing his mouth, and started chewing, slowly, then quickly. It's a popular exercise to warm up the instrument, all this face scrunching, especially for actors, but on a dancer it looks odd. Ugly. The continuation of Martha Graham, but a post-modern Martha, one who no longer makes any sense, whose center has not held, whose tide is unleashed upon the world, and whose proprietor is over the hill, but still one with the dance. A soul without the instrument. A body old before its time.

The Antipodal Dancers made movement based on art installations, and like most small modern dance companies, we had a five-year shelf life. Then everyone moved on. Claire had children. Ellen started scuba diving. I went back to college.

But Ted kept dancing. He started carrying his purple pouch around Manhattan, throwing down his dance floor, and standing still or moving his hips, depending on the ministry needed. God continued to speak to him, but through circular, ecstatic motions, through the language of the yogis, through the language of his body.

Act Ten

"We all have reasons / for moving.
I move / to keep things whole."

—Mark Strand,
"Keeping Things Whole"

Island Rose

I balanced on one leg with the other leg raised at an almost ninety degree angle away from the floor. The ability to balance in such a position came from the sense that my legs pulled away from my body in opposite directions, creating a tension that held my body still in the center. I had learned this basic ability—a foundational movement—from my first dance teacher, Flemming Halby, on Bainbridge Island in Washington State, on the other side of the continent from Martha's Vineyard, where I was now lucky to be rehearsing and performing.

I brought my right leg down, made a quick turn while curving my arms overhead in Fifth position, took a step, and repositioned myself solidly into the same stretched, tilted shape. Every cell of my being reached through and beyond my arms, my legs, the theatre walls. All else was appendage. The center was the whole.

"We'll use this one," said Patricia N. Nanon, founder and artistic director of The Yard, after I finished. I panted a little, although I tried to hide my labored breathing. That ballet training dies hard. Even though modern dancers can show the work of dance, I never wanted anyone to see me pant.

"*Island Rose* is more personal than your other solo," said Patricia. She used a gold-colored pen to make a notation in her notebook.

The other dancers clapped enthusiastically. I took a small curtsy and waltzed off stage. We had all been chosen by audition out of hundreds who applied for the unique opportunity to dance at The Yard on Martha's

Vineyard. In the first week of the residency, the group was choosing which dances to present at the "*. . . by The Yard*" concert the upcoming weekend. It would be the first in a series of performances throughout the summer.

Ten of us were on the Vineyard for Patricia Nanon's session, and we were all pleased. Other downtown dancers frowned at us for doing Pat's work, but we loved it. Pat was sometimes difficult, but only because it was hard for her to convey the movement she wanted. She got frustrated with her body—a dancer should never age—and sometimes took the frustration out on her dancers. But we knew that. We forgave her.

"Good job." Jennifer rolled on two tennis balls in the corner.

Through the open door, I could see the life-sized Steve Lohman sculpture of three women dancing on the lawn. Last summer when I performed on the Vineyard, I had bought a small wire sculpture from Lohman. It was of a dancer doing a *jeté*. I had it hanging in my bathroom.

"Really?" I asked. I pulled on my sweats. It was May, and still a little chilly.

"You'll do great. You're dancing beautifully."

I leaned forward and rubbed my quads. I grabbed the top of my right thigh and shook it a little then rubbed hard up and down my leg. The compliment meant a lot to me. I had choreographed the solo using my interpretation of Mark Morris's movement. I wished, achingly wished, that I had tried for Morris's company rather than spending so much time wrenching my back into the Graham spiral. Morris or Limón was where I should have focused my dancer's life. Not Martha.

Support in the dance world was too rare. At least for me it had been. I'd always had to fight for everything I earned in dance. Everything except that first role all those years ago as "Clara" in *The Nutcracker* with Pacific Northwest Ballet. But after "Clara" came the role of a mouse—the young dancer who plays "Clara" grows up, after all, and the next role for that size of dancer is a mouse or maybe a toy soldier. Then a flower. Maybe snow.

But here at The Yard, it was as if the necessity of taking the ferry from

Wood's Hole to the Vineyard made it possible to leave all the cutthroat competition on the mainland. Or perhaps taking the bus off Manhattan made it possible to leave all competition and memory there—on that island.

Yet my muscles felt the familiar sensation of being on an island. It was something I had mentioned to Jennifer: the sensation of being surrounded by water, comforted by the smell of green grass and dirt mixed evenly with salt spray. Jennifer hadn't understood. Although Manhattan was certainly an island, it was full of manmade smells—not the smells of nature and dirt. Not like here on Martha's Vineyard. And not like Bainbridge Island in Puget Sound across the continent.

I had played with the idea of moving back to Seattle. Staying a dancer and attending the University of Washington. Becoming a dance educator. Or maybe auditioning for the Pat Graney Company in Seattle. The price of the New York City dance world was too exhausting. I needed to finish my college education. I needed to start using my mind, owning my own creative work. I was tired of solving choreographic problems for other people's creative work. Really, I either needed to start choreographing myself, or I needed to get out.

While Pat decided the program order for the "*. . . by The Yard*" concert, Thomas Warfield massaged Hsiu-Ping's neck. As tall as he was generous, Thomas sang every weekend at the Chilmark Community Church. Working with Thomas, it was impossible not to feel, not to be, more fully whole. He brought out the heart in movement. The joy in performance. It was Thomas's ninth season at The Yard. He came back as often as possible. He was a fixture. Soon he would get a job teaching dance at the National Technical Institute for the Deaf at the Rochester Institute for Technology and win a downtown Bessie for a piece choreographed for hearing impaired students. It would get harder for him to come back to the Vineyard each summer.

In 2002, Thomas organized an alumni performance at The Yard, and I came back both to dance and to read a short story. It was a transitional moment. Like this current summer when I was reading Mark Strand's early poetry. I was finally understanding intellectually why I danced—"keeping things whole." I'd always felt the reasons in my body, the desire, yet I was realizing that I didn't need to dance anymore. After dancing for Kevin Wynn, I felt, my body felt, complete somehow. Finished and complete. And not bitter at all. The entirety of feeling was a relief. This would be my last summer dancing.

I unclipped my French barrette and my blonde hair fell almost to my waist. Some modern dancers kept their hair short and sporty, but since I'd originally trained in ballet I kept my hair long.

When I walked into the Side Yard house after the dancers dispersed for the evening, Kun-Yang had already hooked up his electric-stim machine around his knee. His quad muscles jumped slightly. He was sitting on the couch flipping through the latest issue of *Dance Magazine*.

Watching Kun-Yang, I felt my quad muscles tightening up again. A heavy weight filled my legs, my arms, spreading across my lower back.

"Can I borrow that tonight?" I asked.

Kun-Yang nodded and smiled. His face was continually expressive—onstage and off. "With knee crawls," he said, referring to the Graham movement also called knee *bourrées* where a dancer travels rapidly across the stage on the knees, "my knees appreciate the extra help."

"Why put them in your own dance if they hurt so much?" called Jennifer from the kitchen.

"The body directs you to recreate the movement you know," answered Kun-Yang. "So that is what you do."

"Sounds like Martha," yelled Jennifer.

I bent over, touching my nose to my knees. The stretch burned the back of my thighs.

"The body does not lie. Neither did Martha Graham," said Kun-Yang, seriously.

All the dancers teased Kun-Yang that he was an *artiste*. But we all agreed that he was, in fact, an artist. Capital "A."

Kun-Yang had the tensile well-trained muscles of a performer who had trained each and every day for years. There was no middle ground for him. The other dancers knew it. We gave him the space to create perfection. If he cast any of us in his piece, we would do knee crawls without protest.

I patted Kun-Yang's shoulder.

"Need anything?" I asked. "I'm going to the library and to get a slice of pizza."

"One slice," Kun-Yang said, pointing his finger at my stomach. "Cheese will weigh you down. Besides you could take a few off."

Standing in the open doorway between the kitchen and living room, Jennifer blew a kiss at me. I caught it and twirled myself out the door. I'd momentarily forgotten the pain in my quads.

I walked down the gravel driveway and turned right when I hit Middle Road. At Beetlebung Corner, I turned left. If I hurried, I could just make it to the Chilmark Public Library before closing.

℁

After dress rehearsal the next evening, I lay on my bed with a book of Mark Strand's poetry. I was in the top blue room. It had been my friend Heather Harrington's room the year before she joined the Bella Lewitzky Dance Company for the final tour. A long-time dancer of that company, Walter, was with us this summer at The Yard. The blue room was also Patricia Nanon's favorite room in the Side House, which made it seem even more special. A private dressing room. A private room for reflection. For preparing for change.

While holding the book with one hand, reading "Keeping Things Whole," I rubbed a foot with the other, pressing deeply on reflexology points related to my lower back. It was a short poem, but I read it over and over and over, almost as if I were rehearsing a short three-phrase movement set to Strand's poem. Kun-Yang's electric-stim machine pulsed on my quads.

I stopped reading and looked out the window at the fireflies. The fireflies were tiny stage lights flying through the sky. There are no fireflies on the

West Coast. Despite dancing all day long, despite my physical exhaustion, I felt intensely lonely. I wanted to move back to the West. I wanted to live closer to my parents. I wanted to stop striving, stop making my body perform at any cost.

Yet Friday, during opening night performance, I felt rejuvenated, whole. All the worry about trying to get into a dance company, to return to Puget Sound, left me. I was in peak shape, despite the aches, and I was ready to perform my own solo. Mine. My body. My movement. My expression. The sea spray of Martha's Vineyard had worked its way into my muscles. Being on an island again—dancing on an island again—had worked its magic.

I actualized what my first teacher Flemming had taught me all those years before: Energy—meaning—fulfilled every movement, making each moment whole. I stepped into the tilt and directed energy out of every cell of my being. I filled each beat of the music, held each second of stillness. When the audience applauded, I held my hand over my heart. I did a ballerina curtsy—not a modern dance bow.

After watching Kun-Yang's perfection and Thomas's joy finish the evening's performance, I stepped out of the theatre. On an island, surrounded by water, I felt the roots of my beginnings.

I knew that dance creates many reasons for moving.

Act Eleven

"Many dancers simply walk out one day, unwilling or unable to play pretend any longer. Some leave to go to academic schools; the Columbia University School of General Studies, for example. Others decide to look for jobs that are less taxing physically, better paid, and more befitting the personal dignity of an adult."

—Joan Brady,
The Unmaking of a Dancer: An Unconventional Life

Dream of the Minotaur

You enter the theatre. You do not enter through the stage door, through that exalted entryway. There is no guard to tip his hat or raise his chin ever so slightly. There are no aspiring dancers, young ones to play the student parts, who gaze at you, a Chosen One, as you walk by them. You are not dancing in *Diversion of Angels* or in *Acts of Light*.

You enter through the front of the theatre. You buy your ticket for the Martha Graham Dance Company. It is the spring season at City Center in New York City. You have studied the repertory and decided on Program A. *Appalachian Spring* cancels out Program B. *Deaths and Entrances* cancels out program C. And you certainly don't want to see the family matinee, which is Program D, even though you've never seen *Embattled Garden*.

Your favorite solo, *Deep Song,* is not being performed. Your favorite Graham dancer, Sandra Kaufmann, has left the Company, so you won't get to watch her. Sandra continues to teach and perform and choreograph, so you watch her other places, dancing for other choreographers and performing her own work. One project, *Superstrings,* is based on string theory in theoretical physics, and it was conceived with her husband, playwright Michael Bassett, and physicist Brian Greene. It makes you think of the Institute of Physics in London commissioning a piece from choreographer Mark Baldwin to honor Einstein using $E = mc^2$.

You will see Program A: *Errand into the Maze, Sketches from "Chronicle,"* and *El Penitente.* You really want to see Tadej Brdnik in the last; he was in that first Summer Intensive with you. He got a scholarship from the former Yugoslavia. You want to see Alessandra Prosperi, too. You wonder how these people still dance. You know you are now fat.

El Penitente, surprising you, turns out to be your favorite piece of the evening. Simple, spare, direct. You used to hate that piece—so simple, spare, direct. Tadej is strong. Alessandra is quick-footed. You wonder how they do it. Have you forgotten?

You had thought you would love *Sketches from "Chronicle,"* because you love the dancing of Fang-Yi Sheu, but you don't. She's a prima now, and you don't like the mugging for the camera and you cannot stand the ear-high kicked leg, up high in quick succession, as if her crotch was going to split open. You may just be jealous.

Fang-Yi beat you out to join David Hochoy's Company Kaleidoscope in Indiana. You were third in line. She comes from the same school in Taiwan as Hsiu-Ping Chang and Kun-Yang and your favorite Limón dancer Ruping Wang. Fang-Yi turns down the David Hochoy position—he is one of your favorite Graham teachers, or a close second to Steve Rooks, although for consistency and musicality you always took Armgard von Bardeleben's class. The Hochoy position goes to the second in line, whose name you do not remember. Fang-Yi tells you, standing on the street outside of the old Ailey studios, "I'm waiting for the Graham Company." Maybe you've seen *Sketches from "Chronicle"* too many times.

You can't sneak out from backstage and sit in an empty seat. You have to buy your ticket. It is only twelve years since you entered the school. Ten since you left.

It takes ten years to make a dancer, says Martha. Sure does, you think, and then some.

City Center is the theatre with the mosaic tile on the front façade, and in this same place with the red velvet seats, you remember seeing Twyla Tharp's new work for the Company and also Robert Wilson's *Snow on the Mesa.* You actively want to see Martha Clarke's new ballet, *Sueño,* inspired by, or derived from, Francisco Goya's *Los Caprichos*. You like seeing Graham dancers do pieces other than the Graham repertory, but Clarke's piece seems depressingly dark. Given the subject, though, it is honorable that the dancers look as full of air as they do, racing around the stage away from violation.

There is no ticket on reserve for you because of your dedication as an understudy for *Panorama* or your work in the Company office or your endless hours at the school's front desk checking in students for classes and collecting their money. Your friends no longer work as ticket agents or as ushers or as theatre managers, so you are unable to get free tickets that way.

Nevertheless, you do know people who dance tonight. "I trained with them," you say, to no one in particular but mostly to your current boyfriend. He is here, graciously accompanying you to see dance. Since you weren't dating him while you were a dancer, he is excited to see what dance is all about.

You've described the life of the dance, as you call it, and your eyes were so sparkly and full of excitement and your body twitched as you spoke, there was life in those old muscles again, and he became very excited about going to the dance with you. It's an entry, for him, into another part of you. A form of intercourse. He enters a very deep hole left from dance, but it is not one he can penetrate or fill. It disgusts you that he might even try. He probably does not believe you were ever a dancer. Have you mentioned the little problem of fat? You met while at university and are currently engaged in a long-distance relationship that you think will lead to marriage. In reality, neither of you has the guts to break it off, and you lost all your guts when you stopped doing the Graham contraction.

When I left dance, I finished my undergraduate degree at the Columbia University School of General Studies. When I finished my degree, I moved home to Idaho where I worked in the forest, wielding a brush saw and planting tree seedlings. I'd changed my life entirely.

Still, you say, pointing at lines in the program, "I trained with five of these dancers. Three of them were in my very first Summer Intensive." It seems some kind of claim to fame, but you are disgusted with yourself for even saying it. You are also disgusted to discover there is still a hole inside you, a physical void like a black hole. It might be in your heart. It might be in your gut. It happened when you left dance. You realize it might need filling. Your boyfriend won't ever take the place of dance in your heart. He is tied to his mother's apron strings, but you work with his allegiance to his mom because he is gentle and tall. He can lift you. You like anyone who can lift you. Remember Ian Butler? He could lift you. He lifted you in that duet at The Yard. He dances. In Norway. Maybe you should go to Norway.

Before the performance begins, you also discover there's a place inside that is not a hole at all but that is whole. Even if your boyfriend disgusts you at least once a week, you actually like your life now, and you don't struggle with always feeling inadequate: better turn-out, better extension, better abdominal muscles. Every day, there is *not* something that needs to be fixed: Your leg should go a little higher; your psoas isn't working quite right; you've twisted your ankle on the sidewalk when you weren't watching for cracks that might break your mother's back. You've learned that dance is one kind of movement, and in so many ways you feel freer than you ever have in your life. You're over thirty, and you don't give a damn what anyone thinks of you. You like the cackle lines around your mouth and eyes.

There is a dancer's name listed on the poster board in the lobby, and you didn't even know she got into the Company. Momentarily you feel jealous. Out of touch. Then you realize the absurdity of it all, the automatic button of the feeling, and you stop yourself. You are now an adult. You live an adult life. You keep a steady job, you think in your brain, not in your body, you walk around upright instead of crawling across dirty dance floors spotted with dried blood and little bits of ripped skin.

In fact, you've purchased your ticket online before arriving at City Center, and you've flown into the city to see Martha's Company, resurrected after years of legal battles over copyright issues about her dances. You don't know how all these dancers have hung on so long. You like to think it is admirable: this dedication to Martha that you did not have. But you know there is more trouble to come for the Company. The legacy of Martha is such that her fatalism stays with the Company. The long shadow of one man—or woman—and all that.

If you are over dance, if you are resolved about dance, you think none of the old resentments would stir inside. That isn't true. The emotional response is so physical, you almost can't help yourself. You *can* stop yourself. You attend other companies and wonder at the movement and the beauty. You watch Mark Morris and feel sad that you never auditioned for that Company. Now it is all past. You must let go, move on; it no longer matters. You are a beautiful, self-possessed woman who used to dance. You are grateful. You are honestly grateful. You followed your dream. You moved.

Before the show, you stand in the lobby with your ticket and look at the teachers you know and whisper their names to your boyfriend. "There's Donlin Foreman. There's Marianne Bachmann." He does not tell you that he cannot hear you speak because your whisper is so soft. No matter. It does not matter.

Marianne is talking to a young dancer. She is as tall and Teutonic as ever. She is still wearing the same color of red lipstick. You bow your head, so she won't see you. You doubt she would remember you and anyway you don't feel like saying "hello." Immediately you delude yourself that she would remember you. Still, even if she was less than kind to you, you remember how kind Marianne was to your friend whose mother died.

You wonder if the music teacher Ted Dalbotten is still alive. You and Ted stopped writing to each other. He was gentle with you. Ted told you to watch Miki Orihara: "She feels the music in her body. She understands that Graham has musicality; it isn't just about moving before the 'and.'" You wish Miki were performing tonight. You also wish Erica Dankmeyer were performing tonight. The two of you performed together in the park at high noon so many summers ago. Erica made it in, and you want to see her perform *Satyric Festival Song*.

Ted rubbed the rhythm of the music into your skin when you were having difficulty counting it. You still cannot count for shit, and you have to do basic addition by pressing one finger after another. It is not a big problem, because you do not earn big money. You remember there was some syncopated time, and you were about to cry because Ted kept saying you were not feeling the music in your body, but you are a dancer who feels the music in her body, and you couldn't fail at the music class. You had to get your Professional Training Certificate from the Graham Center and get out. The place was making you nuts. You were part of the generation at the school after Martha, yet before the suspension while copyright issues were fought in court. Upheaval and transition.

The usher explains that someone from the Graham Company did not get the program information to *Playbill* in time, so he only has Xeroxes of the programs to hand out. The Xeroxes aren't even stapled. You had wondered why Terese Capucilli was in the lobby handing out glossy cards with pictures of the season's ballets printed on them. In succession, you overhear the usher explain the Xerox situation to each audience member presenting her ticket (the audience has more women than men, though there are a lot of gay men), and you overhear, "Lame"; "Ridiculous"; "Typical"; "Sixty dollars for a ticket with no program." You see a woman with long blonde hair, a tight-fitting bodice, and tight black velvet pants; she says, "Same old Company."

You recognize her, but you bow your head because you don't want her to recognize you. Your mind and what it is saying is becoming slightly histrionic, even to your own sensibilities. You struggle to remember the woman's name who is wearing black velvet. The outfit even looks familiar. She was never a very good dancer, you remember, and she doesn't look as if she is dancing now, and she's sitting right up in the front of the balcony, so she probably isn't working for the Company either. If she were working for the Company and had a comp ticket, she would be sitting farther back in the balcony, or maybe in the orchestra, but not in the expensive seats at the front of the first balcony.

You don't remember her name, but you suddenly remember that she was dating a piano player from class and you thought they got married. In a weird connection, your brother's high school friend Vince Castor, who became an actor and worked as a doorman at a posh hotel on Fifth Avenue, was a friend to this woman's boyfriend. That's how you met Vince again, because you went to hear the Graham accompanist play and sing his folk music at the Bitter End in the Village, and Vince was there.

For Graham, you couldn't decide whether to sit in the orchestra or the balcony, which is where you sat when you watched Baryshnikov in a solo concert, performing Kraig Patterson's work and also performing a solo first performed by Sara Rudner where his heart, Misha's heart, was projected into the theatre as the sound track. You have seen one of the greatest dance barefoot to his own heartbeat.

The decision about where to sit to watch the Graham Company had become as important as the decision used to be about where to take daily dance class after you left the Graham School. You chose to sit in the balcony, because you wanted to see the patterns of movement but you realize, too, that you didn't want to sit in the orchestra pit and face those dancers and former teachers head-on.

Of course, none of the performers can see *you* from the stage. You will not go to the stage door to congratulate them after the performance. You will think about it.

The Chosen Ones, these dancers whom you are about to watch onstage while you sit on your butt in the audience, have danced and danced. Their bodies are not fleeting, nor their careers, and they, unlike you, have had moments where the time onstage became too long when all they wished was to be in their hotel room bathtub or even better home, in their New York City apartment, with their partner, not their dance partner, their lover, together with him or her in bed instead of only hearing the voice on the end of a phone line. There are very few of these dancers. In fact, there are many who have been trained and so many who are worthy and so many who should have, could have, might have been chosen.

True, the best make it to the top, but, wait, it isn't always true. Sometimes only the most persistent make it to the top, if the life of a professional dancer in the United States in the twenty-first century can be considered the top. It's the top of a large heap of dancers who leave dance to live other lives and come to performances and cry as I am about to do.

I am about to cry.

The lights dim. Suddenly, I feel I'm on the wrong side entirely. I never should have stopped dancing. What have I done with my life? I am nothing. A horse put out to pasture. A pig that places last at the fair. A cow with no milk.

But wait, I think, maybe I look even better now because my skin is softer and the outline of my body doesn't look beaten down and internally I don't ache the way I used to ache. Naproxen, four a night while I was dancing, took care of the physical ache, but what about my heart, I want to yell to the audience members. What about what those teachers did to my heart, my belief, my love?

I have lost a lover. That is all. One has panics such as this about ex-lovers. This is the same. This panic right now is simply about having taken one road or the other and never knowing whether I took the road that was right for me. Except, I know. You know. The body retains its intuition even when dance teachers take everything else away. Their screams may burn your skin, but your heart still pumps.

The lights dim, and I am here. I am here with my boyfriend, whom I call my fiancé, although he hasn't proposed. He takes my hand. I want to be left alone.

After this performance, by a length of two months, your excited boyfriend—the same one who thought he could reach inside you through the dance—dumps you. Maybe it was mutual; you aren't sure. He observes that anything difficult that occurs in your life makes you feel fat. As if this is news. You weigh ten pounds more than when you were dancing, but you have no muscle tone. Your abdominals have gone away, not even on vacation, and you can't find them.

You remember performance: You stand backstage at Dance Theater Workshop and hold hands, counting 1, 2, 3, 4, waiting for your entrance when the lights go black and you hurry on in darkness and take your place. Stef stands above you, you crouch below, the stage lights come on, it's a flash, Stef's leg moves, and you move, and suddenly there is only this body, your body, and Stef's body, and the audience is there because you feel them. It's visceral, the audience is in your blood, and you are moving for yourself and your audience and your choreographer, and you don't even think about wanting it to last because you are so *there* you think it will never end. Only later, years later, right now, do you wish the performance had lasted forever because the cliché is that it all goes by so fast, and you dance—most dancers dance—for such a brief moment, yet that moment extends and weaves throughout the rest of your life.

You continue to admire Noguchi's sculptures and his sets for Martha. You remember the Graham teacher Armgard von Bardeleben told you to visit the Noguchi Sculpture Garden, but you never went until a few years ago when you and this same boyfriend took the subway out to Queens to see all that marble and stone.

You still love Barry Flanagan's bronze rabbits. On your way to the theatre tonight you went to visit your favorite Flanagan *Tai Chi Rabbit* at 53rd Street and stood and pointed out the rabbit to your boyfriend. You have moved away from Giacometti sculptures. The figures are in too much pain.

Now you have started to think that artists like Kienholz, with installation work and smells that evoke a place, have more to offer interactively than mere representation, even if that representation is slightly twisted. If you had become a choreographer, you would have created a piece that danced inside a Kienholz room—*The State Hospital,* walls dingy with a single bulb overhead and a bunk bed, maybe, or the brothel *Roxys* that Ed and

Nancy Kienholz reconstructed from Wallace, Idaho, where the madam's head is a feral hog skull. In the latter installation, the dancer could pause, placing one hand on the hog's head and the other on her crotch.

And yet, you love the fleeting, sensual presence of an Andy Goldsworthy installation. His pieces built of natural materials that blow or break with the wind remind you of Eiko & Koma. The two move so slowly they make their dances last. You can visualize dance as less aggressive now, less confrontational, something more beautiful, more hopeful. A slight bend of the knees and an undulation of the body, suggesting the movement of a leaf, the passage of time.

In the Graham performance, you see the way Blakeley White-McGuire leaps, after being raped by men, and her body looks like one wild piece of animal in the air, a flying development of woman, now out of the sea and now on land, now woman in the air above land, reaching the heavens, reaching for heart.

"Extraordinary," you say. "How does she do that?"

The mystery has come back to the dance. Yet you know she does it by practice, by focusing on the muscles and the physical action, not by focusing on the thought of flying. You know she focuses on pushing away from the floor so hard that gravity is momentarily defeated. She does it by years of tending to a body and teasing and pushing it into shape. She does it because she loves to move.

It's a failure of modern dance, you think, theoretically, trying to distance yourself from the emotion of seeing all this Graham technique, to be so married to the floor. It is your training, yet you wonder why you bothered. It is your training, there on stage, being performed by former classmates. You know why you bothered. You *had* to move. You feel all these contrasting emotions, but mostly you feel relieved. You feel sad, in some ways, that modern is still so floor-bound. That suggests to you that you always loved ballet more. This is true. Ballet was your first love. Your first loss. Your way of being in the world is a waltz, sometimes with syncopation, always with the desire for lyricism and beauty. Ballet is so exciting with its trained defiance. Modern now has too much irony, or maybe just cynicism, but it is especially hard to think where so much head-banging and meta-commentary can go but down into dirt and into more earthbound movement.

Perhaps traveling to the core, fighting with the Minotaur, or at least doing it onstage in and around Noguchi's set, is precisely the courage of modern dancers: to face what is unseen, what is hidden, to face fear and to bring it back to the light like Ariadne in *Errand into the Maze*. The heroine shows all that base emotion, or base motion, to the mere mortals watching, whether they are former dancers or not. The Minotaur tonight is Martin Løfnes, and you like him. You like the outline of his muscles. He always chatted with you on the subway.

Some might think I'm jealous because I'm watching and no longer performing, but I don't think that is the case. My body feels too calm to be jealous. The dancers are amazing—incredible movers, truly fantastic, everything is working, muscles and mind and body and spirit; they are alive— but I'm shocked by how angular Graham's movement looks. I'm shocked by how ugly it looks to me now. I'm stunned. I stop crying.

℘

I still dance during the night, in my dreams. Often I don't remember the steps; occasionally, I know all the steps. More frequently, I make them up. Improv, wearing Isadora Duncan tunics.

In my dreams, my body always feels free, with no pain. I never dream of the Minotaur in the form of a raving dance teacher or choreographer. The wooden dance floors are knotty pine with all the ridges sanded smooth.

I see the stage lights, and I begin to move, a waltz, and I am there, center stage, briefly, and then in the chorus, and then with a partner, and my partner is a man or a woman, and then I dance solo.

When I dance solo, I feel my heart beating, and I hear it, too, and I am alive and I am healthy—in mind and body and spirit—and I am so grateful to be moving from stage left to stage right.

Slowly, I walk off the stage. Sometimes I even use the stately Graham walk. And my life begins again.

Act Twelve

"The woman I am is the artist I am. There is no difference."

—Isadora Duncan,
Quoted in Peter Kurth's
Isadora: A Sensational Life

Attending a Wedding: Paris

The first wedding invitation arrives by e-mail. "Isn't life crazy?!" writes Stef and attaches a photo of herself and her lover Guillaume, a cinematographer:

> Written on his white forearm: "Will you marry me?"
> Written on her brown forearm: "Yes!"

In the photo, Stef and Guillaume are snuggled together in bed, smiling at the camera. Guillaume looks handsome in a very classic way, but his hair is slightly messy. Stef's hair is crinkly and enormous—she's let it grow since moving to Europe. They are in Paris, in their apartment. Stef is an American in Paris. Guillaume is Parisian. The French-English dictionary is tossed to the side as if no longer needed.

Stefanie's second wedding invitation arrives at my parents' house in northern Idaho in a square purple envelope with twelve cents postage due. The invitation includes French and English: *Stefanie and Guillaume would like to invite vous à leur mariage.*

There is a small color Xerox map with directions to the *quai* to board *le love boat* for a tour of the *Seine.* Everyone is invited.

I have no money to pay for the plane fare.

"Listen," says my father. We are sitting in our northern Idaho garden, drinking tea, looking up at Scotchman Peak. There's a small circle of snow left near the craggy top. Yet the mountains have a spring light to them, which makes the evergreen forests look as if they are starting to open to a summer heat that hasn't yet arrived. "You've worked so hard, and you've hardly let us help you at all. Let us give you this trip."

I want to disagree with my parents. They've helped me a lot, giving me a place to live at various times in my life. The joke—except it is true—is that in between careers, I always move home to help with the forest. To date, I've planted almost two-thousand seedlings in our family forestland. Paris and New York City, where I met Stef, seem very far away. I want to go to my friend's wedding. "Thanks, Dad," I say. It's settled.

In the old red barn, I find all the costume boxes I've stored over the years. There was the baby ballerina phase, the theater phase, the phase where I made a lot of money doing television commercials, the teaching dance phase, and, finally, the dancing phase. Recently there was the academic phase, and now I am in the forest phase. Stefanie is my friend from the New York City dancing phase. I've saved all my costumes. All my different lives. I am too young and too old for so many different lives.

I find a retro-fifties dress with a blue bow under the bust. The dress, essentially a rectangle shape, has an overcast blue color with portions that are unevenly faded. An outer lace layer covers the taffeta. I pull off my sweatshirt top, pull on the dress over my pink sweatpants, and run out of the barn and into the field where my mother tends columbines in a small circular garden surrounded by rocks we'd hauled over from the creek.

"Mom, look, I found a retro dress to wear to the wedding!"

A few purple columbines, which had already bloomed, frame her face. After a moment, she stands up. "And the running shoes? Are those retro?"

I look down. My body has widened since I'd stopped dancing. No dancing, no marriage, no children. I'm amazed at my mother's patience with her daughter.

The next day, my mother drives me to a boutique called Northern Blue Clothing in Sandpoint, Idaho and explains the entire situation to Barry, the store co-owner.

"Retro material is fine," says Barry, "but not retro style." Barry fits me in a sleek black top with light green-colored stripes down the side and a tight-fitting pair of black pants.

"I would never wear something like this," I say.

"You should start," says Barry. "Time to reevaluate."

I think of Stefanie cuddled in her lover's arms. She's moved forward, physically, mentally, and she's my inspiration. She doesn't give a damn whether I wear retro or not, whether I'm fat or thin—she just wants me at her wedding.

Two months later, my first day in Paris, I wear Barry's sleek black outfit. Because the buildings are older, and not as tall or imposing as they are in New York City, even with the language difference, Paris feels more welcoming than the familiar terrain of New York. Stef and I and two of her friends, Pam and Ayo, go shopping at Etam, a store near the *Place de la Bastille.*

Etam is a sexy store, with lingerie in the windows. The simplicity of the underwear hanging on steel wires makes it look like art made out of everyday function—something like Picasso's *Bull's Head,* which is made of a bicycle seat and handlebars and hangs in a museum within walking distance from this store.

Stef needs a thong to wear with her wedding dress. Ayo and Pam designate me to announce our surprise.

"Girl, this is your bridal shower," I say. "Buy what you want. Don't even look at the price. Find yourself a love string to wear for your new husband."

A tiny smile forms at the corners of Stef's mouth.

"Okay, Hollywood," Ayo says, using a pet name for Stef, "let's get busy." She has the brusque, clipped talk of someone used to living in New York. She waves her hand in the air as if setting 4/4 time.

Ayo wears shorts made of white terry cloth, the white a sharp contrast to her black skin, and a tight tank with another shirt loosely over the top. On her feet, she wears un-laced, white, faux-fur tennis shoes. She carries a tiny little bag tucked right into her armpit.

We find a long white negligee that flows off Stefanie's hips and moves silky sweet when she walks. Stef poses against the door of the dressing room. Ayo and Stef could have been backstage in the dressing room, both still members of Bill T. Jones/Arnie Zane Dance Company, readying themselves for performances in Berlin or New York City or Paris.

"You're getting married," I say for what seems like the hundredth time.

Before the festivities, the confetti still needs to be purchased, and there is some confusion as to how many olives and grapes and cheese to buy for the reception. I am tasked with picking up the wedding bouquet. The florist does not speak English, and the only French I know is to say I don't speak French: *"Je ne parle pas français."* I point at the bouquet and, using crude American jargon, make a thumbs-up sign.

If the wedding had been a dance performance, no detail would have been left to chance so late in the rehearsal process. There would have been confusion and changes and preparation, but there also would have been designated people taking care of those last-minute issues. There certainly wouldn't have been a feel-good atmosphere full of so much gaiety. According to French custom, the bride and groom would have followed their civil service with a church wedding within the next week or two, and they wouldn't have invited everyone to the civil service.

Since they are artists, the boundaries of the stage were not obvious, and it was difficult to tell the entrances and exits. The wedding started in the morning with the civil service, continued with a reception, took a short rest in the afternoon, and reconvened at the Love Boat for dinner and a cruise on the *Seine*.

The sky is an intense blue the morning of Stefanie's wedding. She has an idea that we should all walk down the street together, singing and dancing, to the mayor's office. A boom box takes the place of our singing, and Ayo, wearing a tiny embroidered gold dress, starts us off by strutting along with the box held high over her head.

Stef takes her mother's arm to begin our procession of women. She wears flats for the walk. Everyone else wears high-heeled shoes. We can't dance, much less skip, so we all yell instead. Passersby stop to clap and watch.

Our parade feels more like a carnival than a staged theatrical event, yet there's something fundamentally hopeful about walking down a Parisian street to see my friend married. This is Stef's dream of a village procession to her wedding. She's doing it. Maybe I'll be next.

As we arrive at *Place Léon Blum,* the location of the mayor's office, Guillaume and the men wait across the street. Guillaume looks as if he stepped out of the pages of a nineteenth century novel. He wears tails, and his pants have silk edging on the sides. His white shirt is starched, the collar high. Today, his hair is brushed.

Stef holds herself with assurance, as if she knows that members of an audience will not take their eyes off her. Every muscle has the subtle articulation of a bird's wing, the ability to include an audience inside a moment of movement. Martha Graham might have said that Stef's muscles have developed eyes.

When Guillaume sees Stefanie, he starts to cry.

We all cry. Then we fill the mayor's office. There's a musty smell inside; it's either the velvet-covered seats or because humans have been married inside this room for centuries. There's a feeling that marriage is an age-old event, something to be witnessed and embraced. The vice-mayor, wearing a sash in the colors of the French flag, conducts the service in French and English. In French, he asks the filmmakers to raise their hands, and half the room does. In English, he asks for the dancers to raise their hands, and the other half of the room does. I do, too.

Stefanie's dress had been designed by a costume maker for *l'Opéra Comique* and for the LIDO cabaret on the *Champs-Elysées,* which means that the ensemble has a playful, couture flair. The strapless bodice, a corset made of silk, is a flame-orange color. The skirt has graduated layers of creamy-white chiffon petals. For the day, there is a bustle on the back of the dress; for dinner, the bustle becomes a train; for dancing, the longer train detaches, leaving a short skirt of petals that show off Stef's long brown legs.

In the evening, Stef arrives at *le love boat* for our tour of the *Seine*. Sitting side saddle, she rides behind Guillaume on their silver-colored moped with white chiffon flowers bouncing off the back.

Stefanie's wedding bouquet is a work of art in its own right, full of orchids and lilies and twigs and dried berries. After several of the dancers perform on the top deck, complete with fake gold wigs and Captain Stubing lip-synching, Stefanie tosses her bouquet directly at me. The wind catches it, taking it into the hands of her godmother Priscilla. Priscilla grabs the bundle of flowers. Without missing a beat, she shoves the bouquet into my arms.

"I'm next," I scream. "I'm next."

Perhaps because of this display, throughout the evening an old man at the next table makes eyes at me, raising his bushy eyebrows after each successive swig. Finally, he works up courage to approach me, wobbling as he stands. His breath smells like blue cheese and wine.

Stef's brother Rob helpfully reaches his arm around my shoulder, displacing the elder gentleman's arm, who bows gracefully and leaves.

"He's yours tonight," says Rob.

"Oh boy," I say.

After dinner, I stare at the Eiffel Tower with Jennifer, a dancer I know from New York. Toshiko Oiwa joins us; I've seen her perform many times but never met her. Toshiko has an ethereal, haunting stage presence. I tell her so as the Eiffel Tower lights up. She blushes.

There are people at Stef's wedding whom I have not seen in years. It is part of the inter-weaving of the dance world, and here it is coming together again, albeit briefly, on a barge-like boat on the *Seine*.

We all go downstairs to the dance floor. Stef and her father, a jazz musician, dance to music he composed when Stef was born. Then Guillaume and his mother, a stunning blonde, waltz.

Stef and Guillaume walk away from their parents to link arms with each other. As ABBA's "Dancing Queen" comes on, dancers flood the floor. We are a moving, slinky mass of disco rhythm.

The couple leaves for their week-long honeymoon in Bali at eight o'clock the next morning. I move into their apartment to take care of the cat.

ℰᴐ

Before flying to Paris, I had read *Isadora: A Sensational Life* by Peter Kurth. In an early mode of positive thinking, Isadora used methods of the French psychotherapist, Emile Coué; Kurth writes, Coué was "the author of the first and most famous dictum of mass-marketed positive thinking: 'Every day in every way, I am getting better and better.'" According to Kurth, Isadora reports in her autobiography *My Life* that she used to repeat, "I must find a millionaire! . . . [I repeated it] a hundred times a day, first [as] a joke and then, finally, according to the Coué system, in earnest."

I thought of how I had employed positive thinking in the bathroom of the South Street Seaport, in New York City, when I worked for a posh catering company, visualizing myself performing as a dancer onstage. Actually, the visualizations worked. I had performed onstage as a dancer. And not a bad dancer, I sometimes even allowed myself to think.

The *Cimetière du Père Lachaise* is near Stefanie's apartment, and the only outing I plan for my last day in Paris is a pilgrimage to Isadora Duncan's grave. Isadora Duncan opened the way for Martha Graham and modern dance in America. Agnes de Mille writes, "Isadora cleared away the rubbish. She was a gigantic broom. There has never been such a theater cleaning."

On the way to the cemetery, inspired by the impromptu bridal shower that Pam, Ayo, and I held for Stef, I stop into the Monoprix, a low-budget Target store, and buy myself another bra. I've already spent almost two hundred euros on matching bra and panty sets. The bras in the discount store fit me straight off the rack. Never happens in the United States.

I continue on my way to the cemetery past *Place Léon Blum,* where Stef and Guillaume were married, and up *Rue de la Roquette.* Clouds form overhead. I stand inside one of two entrances to *Cimetière du Père Lachaise* off *Boulevard de Ménilmontant* and stare at the map.

Unlike other people wandering around looking for Jim Morrison or Oscar Wilde or Édith Piaf, I don't want to see anyone other than Isadora. I think ruefully that I don't even know where Martha Graham is buried, but I have always known that Isadora rests in Paris.

I am standing in *Père Lachaise* when the cell phone rings. Stefanie had left it with me and phones from Bali to say all is well—"we are married and happy!"

"I'm on a pilgrimage to Isadora's grave," I say.

I can hear Stefanie's laughter. "Girl, of course *you* are."

The rain ends as I find the crematorium in the center of *Cimetière du Père Lachaise* where Isadora's ashes are held inside an urn and behind a plaque. I've worn my purple polka-dotted scarf in Isadora's honor. I've taken a Calla lily and two dried blackberry twigs from Stefanie's wedding bouquet to leave for Isadora.

I place the flowers under Isadora's plaque:

Isadora

DUNCAN

1877—1927

Ecole du Ballet de l'Opéra de Paris

Duncan's burial service ended with Bach's "Air on the G String." Peter Kurth writes that one of Isadora's close friends said, "She always told me her soul would never leave until it mounted on the strains of that lovely thing."

I remove my sandals and take several photographs of my bare feet with Stef's wedding flowers in front of Isadora's name. In one photograph, I drape my purple scarf over my right foot.

After I leave the cemetery, I cross the street to a *boulangerie* to buy a *pain au chocolat*.

"*Seulement un?*" asks the woman behind the counter.

"*Oui, seulement un.*"

I want something sweet, something to eat right away, something to melt in my mouth.

Coda

"Climaxes, [Merce Cunningham] once said, are for those who get excited over New Year's Eve."

—Joan Acocella,
The New Yorker

Ballerina Blunders & a Few Male Danseurs

Ballerina Blunder # 1

On May 13, 2004, Darci Kistler picked her leotard out of her butt[1] onstage at the State Theater[2], Lincoln Center. Peter Martins, Ballet-Master-in-Chief, was not watching. Darci, Martins's wife, was dancing with Martins's son by a previous marriage, Nilas.[3]

Ballerina Blunder # 2

On May 13, 1980, in the Seattle Opera House (the old Opera House, seating capacity 2,800) Gelsey Kirkland began Odile's thirty-two *fouettés* in *Swan Lake*.[4] Prince Siegfried, Patrick Bissell, stood behind Odile, watching and falling in love. He thought the black swan was the white swan; he didn't realize von Rothbart was tricking him. Bissell wore white tights. Kirkland fell on the eighteenth *fouetté*.[5] Kirkland began again. Fell on the tenth *fouetté*. Kirkland/Odile stood up, looking like a deer caught in headlights. Started again, did three more *fouettés* ending with three *pirouettes*. Finished on the music. Upon Kirkland and Bissell's return to New York City, Bissell was detained on

---

[1] It is not proper ballerina etiquette for her to put fingers on the buttocks and pull down on a tight-fitting leotard. The reasons this is not proper behavior: it does not look pretty; it is not graceful; the ballerina is a figure of ethereal beauty.

[2] Renamed the David H. Koch Theater.

[3] Male danseurs have *cojones*.

[4] Kent Stowell's version at Pacific Northwest Ballet.

[5] The Black Swan should not fall. She is about control and dominance.

charges of possession of cocaine. Kirkland withdrew from her role playing Yuri's lover (acted by Misha) in the movie *The Turning Point*, written by Arthur Laurents, because Kirkland was now Bissell's lover and no longer Misha's. Kirkland and Misha had been actual lovers, and she refused to join him in a cinematic bed. Leslie Browne went on to acclaim in the role. Browne does not perform *fouettés* in the movie.

Male Danseur # 1

In the grand tradition of modern dance choreographers naming their companies after themselves, Paul Taylor left the Martha Graham Dance Company to form the Paul Taylor Dance Company. He performed a duet at one of his first concerts, which was at the 92nd Street Y: Taylor walked to center stage and stood; he did not move; he wore white; a girl sat at his feet. He has very nice thighs. A review appeared in *Dance Observer* signed by LH[6]: a blank box. No text.

Ballerina Blunder # 3

For three years, at the ages of eleven, twelve, and thirteen, Renée E. D'Aoust performed as Clara[7] in Pacific Northwest Ballet's *Nutcracker*. This was Michael Smuin's San Francisco Ballet version—not the later PNB version with fantastical sets by Maurice Sendak and choreography by Kent Stowell. On December 23, 1982, Clara's (Renée's) bow fell out of her hair, which was in ringlets that took two hours to prepare. The blue and white bow landed downstage right in front of the proscenium arch at the very front of the stage. The bow did not fall in the orchestra pit. Noël Mason, the ballet mistress of PNB and a former dancer with Joffrey, yelled at Renée from the wings to pick up the

---

[6] Louis Horst. Paul Taylor's program *7 New Dances* took place on October 20, 1957.

[7] The author's mother also performed as Clara when she was a girl; Susan Saxton D'Aoust performed with the touring company of *Ballet Russe de Monte Carlo*, and the author treasures a photo of lovely young Susan with kind Frederic Franklin bending over to fit a slipper onto her foot (Alexandra Danilova was Franklin's leading lady). Both Susan, in her hometown, and Renée, on tour and also in her hometown of Seattle, performed as Clara in Vancouver, British Columbia. The author later performed as a Mouse and a Flower in Seattle and Vancouver. The author's mother never performed as a Flower. Or a Mouse.

bow.[8] Renée was so in character as Clara, playing with her gift from
Drosselmeyer, Gerard Schwarz conducting, that she did not pick up
the bow. She did not hear the ballet mistress yell her name. The bow
stayed onstage during Snow. After Act I, Ms. Mason had to walk out
in front of the gold curtain and pick up the bow. During intermission,
Renée got in trouble. With two more clips and more hairspray, the bow
was put back in her hair for Act II.

Male Danseur # 2

Donlin Foreman came running downstage left and made an arc to
downstage right. He was sweating so profusely, his right foot slipped
on his own sweat. The sound of his body hitting the stage was louder
than the live music. Foreman fell close to the orchestra pit, but not
in it, and was able to leap up and continue running to the shrine at
the back of the stage. Stravinsky's *Rite of Spring* stops for no one.[9] The
maiden was sacrificed on the right note. Ka-bam. Dead. In Graham's
Rite, the male danseurs wear thong-type costumes over their manly
parts but their butts are all exposed so the audience can see the flexing and power of the gluteus maximus and minimus muscles. It's an
asymmetric row of marching nondescript men who look to be no
more—and no less—than muscle and rhythm. Although dancers are
notoriously clumsy when not dancing and trip all the time, there is
nothing that appears quite as vulnerable as a dancer falling onstage.

---

[8] Noël Mason used to take ballet class with Wendy Perron, the editor of *Dance Magazine,*
and with Marjorie Mussman, when Mason and Mussman were dancing for Robert Joffrey.
Renée later studied with Mussman in New York City, taking her daily ballet class for modern
dancers. It wasn't until the author began researching *Body of a Dancer* that she learned one
of her very first teachers—her favorite as a baby ballerina—and one of her very last teachers—her favorite as a barefoot dancer—used to take class together in New York City. It's a
small world, after all. Rest in peace, Ms. Mussman (1943-2009), rest in peace.

[9] *Rite* did not even stop for the May 29, 1913 Paris audience when it first premiered. The
audience screamed at the dancers, Nijinsky screamed at other dancers backstage, Diaghilev
flashed the house lights, and Stravinsky ranted up and down the aisles.

Ballerina Blunder # 4

Yvonne Bourree raised her arm and pointed her foot. She started running downstage to take a fish dive into the Prince's arms. Every *Nutcracker pas de deux* ends this way. The Sugar Plum Fairy, who previously in the ballet has been independent and self-assured, throws herself through the air and into the arms of the male danseur, who has done nothing but stand and look pretty the whole ballet. Just before jumping, Bourree's foot slipped a little in front of her, the way a foot will slip out when the knee hyperextends backward and the bones pop out of the joint. She stopped. Her prince walked to her, gave her his arm, and together they walked offstage. The middle-aged moms at the State Theater, who had brought their daughters to see *The Nutcracker,* cried harder. Their husbands never opened doors for them anymore. They should never have stopped dancing.

Male Danseur # 3

The First Chamber Dance Company, formed by Charles Bennett (rest in peace), performed a ballet called *Ragtime* to the music of Scott Joplin. Frank Bays, in a pinstripe suit, *sautéed* on one foot. Snap. The sound, in a space in the music, was heard throughout the Seattle Opera House. Frank Bays hopped on one foot offstage into the first wing. He had snapped his Achilles tendon in half. He walked again, but he never performed *Ragtime* again. The First Chamber Dance Company disbanded in 1979.

Ballerina Blunder # 5

Renée E. D'Aoust worked as an administrative assistant in the Barnard Department of Dance. Donlin Foreman (Male Danseur # 2) taught Graham Technique courses at Barnard. For a time, Mr. Foreman was the only male instructor in the Department. Whenever Mr. Foreman arrived, Ms. D'Aoust said under her breath, "The Penis has arrived." During endless departmental meetings, he always said, "Do these meetings really make the world go round?"

Katie Glasner also worked in the Barnard Department of Dance. She was one of Twyla Tharp's company members in the various iterations of Tharp's companies. Twyla Tharp is now known popularly for her Broadway show *Movin' Out,* which uses Billy Joel songs and dance and no recitative (if talking in Broadway musicals can be called recitative). Twyla Tharp wrote in her own memoir that she got to sleep (have sex) with Baryshnikov. Neato.[10] In the hall of Barnard's Annex, Renée E. D'Aoust told Katie Glasner[11] that she and her mom must have seen her perform with Tharp in Seattle circa 1979. D'Aoust was twelve years old. Probably the dance was *The Catherine Wheel.* It's a memorable performance because of the male danseur who came and took ballet class at Pacific Northwest Ballet School. He was so bad. Then onstage that night he was so good. Moral of the story: a male danseur bad in one form of dance might be good in another form of dance. Another moral: always sleep with your leading man.

---

[10] For the record, the author would not have kicked Misha out of her bed, either.

[11] Katie Glasner also appeared in the movie *Hair,* which had choreography by Tharp, and the author watched *Hair* three times the first weekend it opened.

Renée E. D'Aoust

Biographies of a Few Performers & One Movie

Bissell, Patrick: Died of a cocaine overdose.

Bourree, Yvonne: Principal dancer, New York City Ballet. A dancer of light musicality and extraordinary beauty.

D'Aoust, Renée E.: The author. Clara at eleven, twelve, and thirteen for Pacific Northwest Ballet, and a mouse in *The Nutcracker* at age fourteen. Unmarried at forty. Married at forty-one. No eating disorders. Former member of the Antipodal Dancers. As a teen, sat in the Seattle Opera House while Gelsey Kirkland fell.

Foreman, Donlin: Trained at The House of the Pelvic Truth. Formed a company, named Buglisi/Foreman Dance, with his wife, now ex-wife, and now renamed company.[12] Buglisi is also a Graham dancer and likes to glorify Native American rituals in Graham classes.

Louis Horst: Martha's piano man and much more.

Kirkland, Gelsey: At height of career weighed eighty pounds. Had injections in lips to create voluptuous and pout-like quality.

Kistler, Darci: NYCB Principal. Date of retirement: June 2010.

Martins, Peter: Ballet-Master-in-Chief, NYCB.

Misha: Mikhail Baryshnikov. Russian male danseur. Co-founder with Mark Morris of the modern dance White Oak Dance Project. Founder of the Baryshnikov Arts Center.

Taylor, Paul: The author is fond of Taylor's ballet *Company B*. She doesn't care much for his *Rite of Spring*, but she definitely recommends attending a Taylor performance as a first date activity.

The Turning Point: Movie written by Arthur Laurents (rest in peace). Shirley MacLaine and Anne Bancroft star; famous scene about toads where

---

[12] Buglisi/Foreman Dance founders also included Terese Capucilli and Christine Dakin. Jacqulyn Buglisi now runs Buglisi Dance Theatre.

MacLaine and Bancroft end up in a cat fight near the fountain at Lincoln Center. Famous question (paraphrased): "Here's a toad; would you like me to share this toad with you?" Red carpet treatment in movie for Leslie Browne who for years remained in ABT's chorus.

Concise Glossary of Dance Usage[13]

Fish dive: Ballerina jumps like a flying fish into male danseur's arms.

Fouetté: Must do at least thirty-two to perform Odette/Odile in *Swan Lake.* Nina Ananiashvili does more.

Pas de Deux: Dance for two. In romantic ballet, the *pas de deux* is for a male and a female. In Mark Morris ballets, the *pas de deux* is often for two men. In *Dido and Aeneas,* Mark Morris himself played Dido.[14]

Pirouette: The standing leg is straight while raised leg is bent with toe at the knee, forming a turned-out triangle to the side. This forms the position of *passé.* Then the dancer turns, spins, and this makes the *pirouette.*

Sauté: Not the process of frying onions, but a small hop on one foot.

---

[13] Ballet vocabulary forms a lineage directly back to the court of Louis XIV (1643-1715).

[14] In the time of Louis XIV, men wearing wigs and masks played women's roles.

Two Useful New York City Addresses for the Aspiring Performer

Tiger Information Systems: Temporary agency in New York City that hires dancers. Address: 120 Broadway, 28th Floor, New York, NY 10271. Phone: (212) 412-0600. Fax: (212) 385-3754.

Tai Chi Rabbit: Barry Flanagan (rest in peace) statue of bronze three-foot rabbit in Tai Chi pose. Found at outdoor garden in between 52nd and 53rd Streets near Seventh Avenue. Looking down the rabbit hole and staring at bronze rabbit, useful for inspiration and centering qualities.

A Note About Gratitude

If you are a dancer, you will know why we dance—despite setback and physical pain and body abuse. You will see through the humiliations and understand the satisfaction of moving, of being bound and free, contained and expressive, and you will know the gratitude that I feel as a former dancer. If you are not a dancer, you might wonder why we do it—with all those humiliations, with all the pain. It is more than breath; it is expression; body movement is a dancer's language. Might the field be less brutal? Yes, but the language available is the language that must be used.

Still, it needs to be said clearly that I am grateful for the ecstasy of the dance. It is my blood memory; my body is still my shrine. But my body is no longer my identity, and for that, I am grateful. Beyond that, I am grateful to have moved, to have been controlled and free within the bounds of the dance studio, the black box theatre, and the proscenium stage. I am grateful for the medium of body language. I am grateful to have pointed my toe, raised my leg to my ear (well, not quite to the ear), and opened my arms to God. A waltz, or a walk, or a step—and now standing still—I am here.

When I dream, I am dancing solo: I am so grateful to be moving from stage left to stage right. After each performance, slowly, I walk off the stage. Sometimes I even use the stately Graham walk. And my life begins again.

[Curtain Down.]

About Renée E. D'Aoust

Trained on scholarship as a dancer at Pacific Northwest Ballet and later at the Martha Graham Center for Contemporary Dance, Renée E. D'Aoust performed on proscenium stages and in black box theaters. Now as a writer, she has numerous publications and awards to her credit, including a fellowship from the National Endowment for the Arts Journalism Institute for Dance Criticism at American Dance Festival, support from the Puffin Foundation, and grants from the Idaho Commission on the Arts. D'Aoust holds degrees from Columbia University and the University of Notre Dame. For more information, please visit www.reneedaoust.com.

Books from Etruscan Press

The Disappearance of Seth | Kazim Ali
Drift Ice | Jennifer Atkinson
Crow Man | Tom Bailey
Coronology | Claire Bateman
Cinder | Bruce Bond
Peal | Bruce Bond
Toucans in the Arctic | Scott Coffel
Nahoonkara | Peter Grandbois
Confessions of Doc Williams & Other Poems | William Heyen
A Poetics of Hiroshima | William Heyen
Shoah Train | William Heyen
September 11, 2001 American Writers Respond |Edited by William Heyen
As Easy As Lying | H. L. Hix
Chromatic | H. L. Hix
First Fire, Then Birds | H. L. Hix
God Bless | H. L. Hix
Incident Light | H. L. Hix
Legible Heavens | H. L. Hix
Lines of Inquiry | H. L. Hix
Shadows of Houses | H. L. Hix
Wild and Whirling Words: A Poetic Conversation | H. L. Hix
Art Into Life | Frederick R. Karl
Free Concert: New and Selected Poems | Milton Kessler
Parallel Lives | Michael Lind
The Burning House | Paul Lisicky
Synergos | Robert Manzano
The Gambler's Nephew | Jack Matthews
Venison | Thorpe Moeckel
So Late, So Soon | Carol Moldaw
The Widening | Carol Moldaw
Saint Joe's Passion | JD Schraffenberger
Lies Will Take You Somewhere | Sheila Schwartz
American Fugue | Alexis Stamatis
The Casanova Chronicles | Myrna Stone
White Horse: A Columbian Journey | Diane Thiel
The Fugitive Self | John Wheatcroft

Etruscan Press is Proud of Support Received From

Wilkes University

Youngstown State University

The Raymond John Wean Foundation

The Ohio Arts Council

The Stephen & Jeryl Oristaglio Foundation

The Nathalie & James Andrews Foundation

The National Endowment for the Arts

The Ruth H. Beecher Foundation

The Bates-Manzano Fund

The New Mexico Community Foundation

Founded in 2001 with a generous grant from the Oristaglio Foundation, Etruscan Press is a nonprofit cooperative of poets and writers working to produce and promote books that nurture the dialogue among genres, achieve a distinctive voice, and reshape the literary and cultural histories of which we are a part.

etruscan press
www.etruscanpress.org

Etruscan Press books may be ordered from

Consortium Book Sales and Distribution
800.283.3572
www.cbsd.con

Small Press Distribution
800.869.7553
www.spdbooks.com

Etruscan Press is a 501(c)(3) nonprofit organization.
Contributions to Etruscan Press are tax deductible
as allowed under applicable law.
For more information, a prospectus,
or to order one of our titles,
contact us at books@etruscanpress.org.